STREET FISHER
LIVING ON MISSION FOR GOD

MATTHEW 4:19

KEVIN RIORDAN

Acknowledgements

This book is dedicated to my father, Chuck Riordan. You grabbed a hold of the Savior's garment, and you never let go. Thank you for giving me Jesus.

Contents

Foreword

The calling of a fisherman to the forgotten streets of cities and nations is perhaps the highest call to the world's largest harvest field. Kevin Riordan's passion for lost souls brands him the term "Street Fisher" as it unearths treasures out of darkness, ravaging Satan's kingdom, as ordinary streets turn gold as heaven touches earth.

No one is exempt from God's liberating power as Kevin's gift of healing and deliverance leads him into restaurants, stores, and even the internet where miracles happen, proving there's no distance with God.

Streetfisher: Living on Mission for God tells how Kevin's powerful gifting is used as bait to ultimately hook people to Jesus, the One who touches them and loves them no matter what.

Through many years of testing and refining, you will read Kevin's story of God's faithfulness of using him, proving we have God's treasure in earthen vessels. His transparency and being honestly real earns him the right to tell everyone, "Now God wants YOU to lay hands on the sick and see them recover. Watch what He will do." What a powerful book.

Bill Yount, Speaker & Author
Some Hear Thunder... I Hear a Roar!
www.billyount.com

Introduction

I was on my way home from work. As I drove through Clarion, PA, I saw a young girl of about twenty walking down the street. I drove past her and suddenly felt a prompting from the Lord to go speak with her. His voice did not come thundering into my car saying, "Go speak with that girl with the red shirt!" It was a feeling I had, a quick connection that I made with her as I saw her. However, I ignored it and kept going. I began to feel an uneasiness in my spirit that was increasing as I continued to drive on. I just wanted to get home. I had a long day, and I was tired. The uneasiness got to a point where it was unbearable. I knew that I needed to pull over and talk with her about Jesus.

I had a big problem. There was no place to park my car except in a parking lot that seemed to be a hundred miles away from where she now was.

I parked my car, got out and began to jog after her. I quickly realized that my jog wasn't going to do it; she was losing me. I began to run as fast as my little five foot four legs would carry me. Did I mention that it was about ninety degrees?

I figured that I'd run halfway, call out to her, she'd stop, and I'd walk the rest of the way. It didn't quite happen that way though. I called out to her, but she just kept going. As I ran, I had a dialogue with God. "God, I sure hope you're in this, because if you're not, I'm going to look like a fool! I don't even know what I'm going to say!" I got within fifty feet of her and called out to her again. Again, she just kept going. I got a little closer and noticed that she had ear buds in her ears. I didn't want to freak her out by running up upon her, so I crossed the street and was running alongside her, waving my hand to get her attention, all the while I'm thinking, "Boy, I sure look like a crazy person!"

I managed to get her attention. She gave me a look, like I had 6 heads, and for good reason!

Here I am, a complete stranger who just chased her down, shirt half untucked, sweat pouring off my face, and unable to speak due to being unable to breathe. Panting, I managed to get the words out, "I swear that I'm not weird! I was driving past you and I felt so strongly that God wanted me to stop and tell you how much He loves you and wants a relationship with you." I pointed to my car, which was quite a distance away. I said, "He had me run to catch up with you to tell you that." As I said this, I noticed that she began to tremble, and tears began to fill her eyes. I asked, "Why are you trembling?"

She said, "I didn't grow up in a church, I have never read the Bible, yet for the last month I have not been able to get God out of my mind. I know nothing about Him, yet I am being drawn to Him. As a matter of fact, the thought that was going through my mind moments before I saw you was that I need a relationship with God! Now here you are chasing me down from a mile away to tell me that God loves me and wants a relationship with me? This is not a coincidence! I need God in my life!"

I told her about Jesus. I explained to her what Christ did on the cross for her and how to receive salvation. I then led her in a prayer to accept Jesus as her Savior. We both walked away from that encounter completely in awe of a God who is in hot pursuit of broken humanity, in awe of a God who is working behind the scenes, orchestrating situations, and positioning those who are His own to reach those who are not.

God wants you to know that you have been hand-selected to lead people into a relationship with Him. You have been called to heal the sick and cast out demons! God is not looking for the spiritual superstars. He is not looking for those who are perfect, with perfect theology, and perfect pasts. God is looking for someone who is willing to step out of their comfort zone and to make His mission their mission. He is looking for those who will choose to answer the call to GO.

For those who will make this their lifestyle, you will find that life becomes an adventure. Going to the grocery store to buy milk and bread becomes a mission trip. Stopping at a gas station becomes a revival service. God has invited you to go on a fishing adventure. The location for this trip is the streets where you live. The bait that we use is the love of God. Our targeted "catch" is the hearts of men. The Lord is still asking the questions: whom shall I send, and who will go for us? Will it be you? If you accept His invitation, a wonderful adventure awaits.

Chapter 1

My Little
Yellow Bike

When I was six years old, I went to a yard sale with my mom. As I got out of the car, I saw her in the distance. There she was - a golden beauty. It was a little yellow chopper-style bicycle with a number 7 on the handlebars. I had to have her! And so, the begging commenced. "Please mom, please. I'll be good. I'll do this. I'll do that." My mother, worn down by my empty promises and annoying begging, finally forked up five bucks. I was now the proud owner of the coolest stinking bike anyone had ever seen! There was one problem. I had no clue how to ride a bike!

Every day I would come home from school, and the first thing I would do is go out and sit on my bike. I dreamed of riding it, hair blowing in the wind as I cruised off into the sunset. I would study the bike. I knew every inch of it. There were times that I would psyche myself up to push the pedals and attempt to ride it. However, the fear of crashing would quickly squash my urge. One day, I came outside to find that my little yellow bike was gone! Someone ripped me off! My heart sank. I never rode my little golden beauty.

You may be asking, "So why the yellow bike story?" I think many of us treat sharing our faith in the same way I viewed my little yellow bike. We are enamored by evangelism. We love hearing stories of people coming to Jesus, miraculous healings, dramatic deliverances. We read books about it, go to conferences and seminars. We study it to death. We dream about doing cool things for Jesus. We psyche ourselves up to step out. We see our evangelism target, and we put our foot on the pedal. We want so badly to open our mouth. We walk towards them, heart pounding, palms sweating, thinking, "This time I'm going to do it!" Suddenly, fear of crashing overtakes us. "What if they don't want to hear what I have to say? What if they ask me a question that I can't answer? What if I don't know enough of the Bible?"

Feeling defeated, we take our foot off the pedal. I could dream of riding my bike, and I could study my bike all I wanted, but I would never learn to ride it until I actually got on it, told fear to shut up, pushed the pedals, and attempted to ride it! The same is true with evangelism. We can study it, and dream of it, but we will never become less uncomfortable with it, and more effective at it, unless we step out and do it!

The words in this book will only take you so far. The best teacher truly is experience. You can be sure that as you step out, the Holy Spirit will step with you.

Mark 16:20 "And they went out and preached everywhere, while the Lord worked with them and confirmed the message by accompanying signs."

The more you are willing to step out, the less awkward you will feel. You will see His power made perfect in your weakness. But first things first: get on the bike, put your foot on the pedals, and push!

Chapter 2

The Baby Bird

I was six months old in the Lord when I had my first experience with street ministry. I was going to a little church in Poughkeepsie, NY called "The Bread of Life". Years earlier, this church was formed out of a street ministry. A group of men would come up from the suburbs to the city to share the gospel. Many were saved on the streets. In fact, so many were saved, that they decided to plant a church. Twenty years later there was little evangelism taking place outside of a Wednesday night meal/Bible study that was put on for the homeless and anyone else who needed a meal.

I clearly remember Pastor Charles making the announcement that the Lord had spoken to him about getting back to their roots. He said, "I feel that the Lord is calling us back to the streets to evangelize. Who's going to join me?" Hands went up all over the room. Not wanting to look un-spiritual, I put my hand up, though I had no intention of doing street ministry. A plan was set. The following week we would do role-playing, and the week after would be go time.

The big night arrived. Pastor Charles was a large man with a thick Tennessee accent. He stood up and said, "Okay, it's time to go. Who's coming?" Silence. Crickets. He began to go to individual people. He asked if they were still planning to go. Everyone had an excuse as to why they could not go. As he made his way to me, I realized that everyone else shot him down and I was the last person he had to ask. I was the make it or break it guy. I was the deciding factor. If I don't go, nobody goes. He came over to me and looked at me with his big brown puppy dog eyes. With his southern drawl, he asked, "Keeevin, are you gonna go out on the street tonight?" On the inside of me, a lion roared, "NOOOOOOOOOOO", but from my lips squeaked the word "yes." I felt sick. I wanted no part of street ministry, but God had another plan.

As we were walking out of the church, Pastor Charles assured me that I wouldn't have to talk to anyone. He told me to just listen to him and when I felt that I was ready, I could jump in. So here we were out on Main Street in Poughkeepsie. Pastor Charles was talking to a young guy, and I was standing on the corner trying to make it look like I was hailing a cab. Suddenly I heard those fateful words, "Hey Keeevin, come ova here and take one of these tracts and give it to this lady coming up the street."

Looking back on the encounter, I get the picture in my mind of a newly hatched baby bird. In the nest under mommy bird's wing, the baby bird doesn't have a care in the world. Mommy bird goes off and finds a worm and comes back to the nest and drops it down the baby bird's throat. Life is good for baby bird. Then one day, mommy bird decides to kick baby bird out of the nest, because it's time to learn to fly! That night, I was baby bird.

In my mind, I was thinking, "What about our deal? I don't feel comfortable yet!" But not wanting to look un-spiritual, I went over and took the tract from him. As the woman approached, my knees were knocking, and my heart was pounding so hard I thought it would explode! I held out the tract and said something unintelligible. I meant to say, "Can I give you something to read about Jesus?" but my tongue was momentarily paralyzed. Without looking at me, she snatched the tract out of my hand and kept going.

It was at that moment that I fell in love with evangelism. I watched her reading the tract as she walked down the street. Just then, I got the revelation that what I had done was eternal. Everyone will eventually die, and everyone will go somewhere. If that woman repented and gave her life to Christ, she will praise God for all eternity in heaven as she remembers all the people that God sent to her with the message of the gospel. However, if she never repents, in hell she will remember all the people that God sent to her with the message of the gospel, and it will be added to her torment forever. It was at that moment on Main Street in Poughkeepsie, NY that the Lord lit a fire in my heart to share the gospel. That was the only time Pastor Charles went out on the street. I never stopped.

I think back to that first night on the street. I never in a million years would have thought as I was walking out of the church that night that I was stepping, or rather being shoved, into the destiny that God had for me. Prior to that night, I had no idea there was a gift in me. I had resigned myself to the belief that I could not do evangelism. Had I not been forced out of the nest that fateful night, I would have gone on believing that this ministry was not for me. I think many in the church believe they cannot be effective in sharing Jesus, so they never try. As it pertains to sharing Christ, the word "can't" is a paralyzing word. The truth is that you "**can** do all things through Christ who gives you strength!" (Philipians 4:13).

I have purposed to share the gospel of Jesus Christ every single day. I have incorporated it into my life. A follower of Jesus is **who I am** and giving Him away is **what I do**. Over the last twenty-one years, I have led famous rock stars to Jesus. I have seen atheists become believers. I have seen big tough guys weep as the love of the Savior is revealed to them. I have seen God heal thousands of people and seen thousands more set free from demons. The Lord has given me the great honor of participating in reconciling the hearts of multitudes back to the Father.

The large majority of what I have seen God do has not been done in churches, but on the streets where the lost live, shop, and work. Everywhere there are people, there is a God encounter waiting to happen. Every believer has been called to this. The question is not, "will God use you?" The question is, "are you willing to allow Him to use you?"

Chapter 3

The Maniac Evangelist

God has given me the wonderful opportunity to travel around the world to minister in various churches. The church loves stories of amazing healings and dramatic deliverances, leading to a person receiving salvation. We dream of healing the sick, casting out demons, and leading people to Jesus. Unfortunately, most of the church has the belief that God would never use them in this way. The prevailing thought is that if someone is going to be healed, delivered, or saved, that this will only happen through an apostle, prophet, pastor, teacher, or evangelist. In some churches, this is taught. In most instances, we just grow up believing that the man with the microphone does the "important" ministry, while our ministry is cleaning the toilets, changing diapers, or making the coffee. This mindset has stunted Kingdom growth in a big way. The primary job of the apostle, prophet, pastor, teacher, and evangelist (the five-fold ministry offices) is not to do all the work, but to train the body to do the work of the ministry.

"So Christ himself gave the apostles, the prophets, the evangelists, the pastors and teachers, to equip his people for works of service, so that the body of Christ may be built up" (Ephesians 4:11-12).

The day of the rock star minister has got to end! The Lord has called us all to be participants in what He is doing on the earth. The reality is that no born-again believer is just average, but we are all rock stars because of the Holy Spirit's indwelling presence. Contrary to what some ministers portray, and what most believers believe, there is no hierarchy in the Kingdom of God! Yes, there are different jobs that we have been given; but we have all been given the same task of advancing the Kingdom.

Matthew 28:18 says, "And Jesus came and said to them, 'All authority in heaven and on earth has been given to me.'"

Jesus, being the head of the church, was given all authority in heaven and earth. The body does not walk independently of the head. If the head has been given all authority in heaven and earth, then so were you, because you are part of His body. In addition to having all authority, if you are born again and filled with the Holy Ghost, then all the power that Christ walked in is on the inside of you! So right now, as it stands, you have everything you would ever need and more to decimate Satan and his demons; but you must believe it and choose to walk in it.

I have led many teams to Honduras on ministry trips. When I select people to join me, I look for people with a burning passion to see God release His Kingdom through their lives. Most of them, prior to the trip, have not had extensive ministry experience and subsequently have been limited in seeing God move through them. For a week straight, the team is immersed in evangelism, healing, and deliverance ministry. On the first night of ministry, they step out on shaky legs and God heals and delivers through them! I love the van ride back to the hotel, as the team excitedly shares their stories of what they saw God do! Faith has been built and now it is game on!

From then on, when the people come forward, they believe wholeheartedly that God will perform His Word, and He does! The result is that those who had not seen many healings or deliverances are now seeing many healed and delivered. As the week progresses, the team no longer hopes that God will use them, they wholeheartedly expect it. Many times, when the team returns to the United States, they continue to function in healing and deliverance at a high level. What has changed? They left the United States with the same Holy Spirit that they returned with. The only thing that changed was that they now had a confidence in the Holy Spirit's power that dwells within them, and God's willingness to work through them.

God is not up in heaven looking down on His church saying, "I'm willing to use you three over here, but not you two." Why do so many believe that God has His elite group of Christians, and the rest of us are only regular Joes? This is a lie straight out of the pit of hell!

In Mark 16:15-18, Jesus said, "*Go into all the world and preach the gospel to every creature. The one who believes and is baptized will be saved, but the one who does not believe will be condemned. These signs will accompany those who believe: In my name they will drive out demons; they will speak in new languages; they will pick up snakes with their hands, and whatever poison they drink will not harm them; they will place their hands on the sick and they will be well."*

Notice that nowhere does it say, "These signs will follow the theologian or the slick-talking, polished evangelist." What it does say is that if you are a believer and are willing to put yourself out there to win the lost, heal the sick or cast out devils, then God will use you. The truth is that God wants to use you more than you want to be used!

One of the biggest lies that holds believers back is the belief that they are the sum total of their past. They live under a cloud of shame, as the enemy is all too happy to remind them often of where they have been, who they were, and the things they've done. Shame screams: "You are no good and un-usable!" This feeling of unworthiness robs confidence; without confidence, you will never step out. God loves to use people whom we would least expect Him to use. This is demonstrated clearly in the story of the demoniac.

Luke 8:26-39 says, "*So they sailed over to the region of the Gerasenes, which is opposite Galilee. As Jesus stepped ashore, a certain man from the town met him who was possessed by demons. For a long time this man had worn no clothes and had not lived in a house, but among the tombs. When he saw Jesus, he cried out, fell down before him, and shouted with a loud voice, 'Leave me alone, Jesus, Son of the Most High God! I beg you, do not torment me!' For Jesus had started commanding the evil spirit to come out of the man. (For it had seized him many times, so he would be bound with chains and shackles and kept under guard. But he would break the restraints and be driven by the demon into deserted places.)*

Jesus then asked him, 'What is your name?' He said, 'Legion,' because many demons had entered him. And they began to beg him not to order them to depart into the abyss.

Now a large herd of pigs was feeding there on the hillside, and the demonic spirits begged Jesus to let them go into them. He gave them permission. So the demons came out of the man and went into the pigs, and the herd of pigs rushed down the steep slope into the lake and drowned.

When the herdsmen saw what had happened, they ran off and spread the news in the town and countryside. So the people went out to see what had happened, and they came to Jesus.

They found the man from whom the demons had gone out, sitting at Jesus' feet, clothed and in his right mind, and they were afraid. Those who had seen it told them how the man who had been demon-possessed had been healed. Then all the people of the Gerasenes and the surrounding region asked Jesus to leave them alone, for they were seized with great fear. So he got into the boat and left.

The man from whom the demons had gone out begged to go with him, but Jesus sent him away, saying, 'Return to your home, and declare what God has done for you.' So he went away, proclaiming throughout the whole town what Jesus had done for him."

This man was the town crazy. Everyone knew of him, and everyone feared him. He was famous as the naked lunatic who lived in the cemetery, that is until he had a run-in with the Deliverer! In a matter of moments, Jesus set him free from thousands of demons and restored him to his right mind.

At the end of the story, this man begged to stay with Jesus. But Jesus had other plans for him! Jesus then gives this man his marching orders. Jesus instructed him to go home and evangelize his town. There are some key things here that must be noted. Jesus did not sit him down for a set amount of time until He was sure he could trust him. Nor did Jesus make him take a six-month discipleship course to make sure he had all of his doctrinal ducks in a row. Jesus didn't put any of the demands on him that some pastors place on their people before they are allowed to minister.

I'm sure there were some things that needed to be done in this man's heart. More than likely, he was rough around the edges. Jesus saw a passion and a fire in him and wanted to strike while the iron was hot! By sending him home to tell his story, in essence Jesus was saying, 'Go despite your ugly past and awful reputation. Go, despite your imperfect heart. I know that there is still much for you to learn theologically, and maybe you'll make some messes, but I see the gold that's in you. I know the work that has been done in you! I trust you, now go!'

Like the demoniac, your past has not disqualified you from ministry, but your broken past that was healed is the thing that qualifies you for excellent ministry. This is the beauty for ashes that was promised to you. Your past brokenness is now gold to be given away! If God can trust a maniac to be His mouthpiece, He can trust you!

I'd like to conclude this chapter with a prophetic word that I received a few months ago:

While praying I saw a box in the middle of a church sanctuary. This box was wrapped in chains. Suddenly the box exploded, and the Holy Spirit burst from the box and filled the sanctuary. Suddenly I was outside of the church. I saw another explosion. The Holy Spirit exploded out of the roof. He began to fall on disreputable-looking people. Before falling on them, there was a darkness in the center of their chests. When the Spirit of God fell on them, that darkness turned to gold. I saw them run to other disreputable people.

Those with the gold in their chests reached into their chest and pulled out gold and gave it to the others. Suddenly the darkness that was in them became gold. And they began to run and do the same. I heard the Lord say, "Let the weak say I am strong, let the poor say I am rich! My power is perfected in your weakness. Those who are weak will demonstrate my power. Those whom the religious overlook, I am busting out of religious boxes; I'm bursting religious chains."

Chapter 4

The Great Chess Game and Guns 'n Roses

was driving home from a meeting one evening and took a wrong turn. I was lost. I had no clue as to where I was. Finally, I found a convenience store. I pulled in to try to figure out where I was. I was sitting in my car with the windows open, punching my location into my GPS, when suddenly an SUV pulled into the parking space beside me. A woman got out of the passenger side and went in. There was a man in the driver's seat, and he was listening to the radio. The song, "November Rain" by Guns 'n Roses came on. So here I am enjoying the opening piano of the song when suddenly I heard a sound that sounded like a cat in heat. The man in the SUV loudly began to belt out the song. He sounded awful. He was giving it his all, and I could tell that he thought he sounded amazing. The Word instructs us to be all things to all men to win them, so at that point, I became a liar for Christ.

I leaned forward and got his attention and said, "Hey dude, you sound good!" He replied, "Yeah. I know. I love Guns 'N Roses." Next thing I know, he and I were swapping stories of when we saw the band in concert. As we spoke, God began to speak to me. In my mind I heard the words: "Right leg pain from below his hip, to his ankle."

I said to him, "This may sound crazy, but do you have pain in your right leg?" He told me that he had been in a motorcycle accident 15 years ago, resulting in his entire right leg being crushed. He told me that his leg was now made of titanium. I asked him about his pain level. He said his pain was constant and severe but there are days where it is off the charts. He asked me how I knew about his leg. I told him, "I don't, but I know the One who knows everything about you, and He told me. God wants to show you that He sees you and that He loves you." I could see by the look on his face that these words affected him powerfully.

I told him I felt that God would heal him if he would let me pray for him. He agreed, and we both got out of our vehicles. There was a bench in front of the store that I asked him to sit on. I felt that he had a leg shorter than the other. I held up his legs side by side and sure enough, his left leg was an inch and a half shorter. As I was comparing his legs side by side, his wife came out of the store to find some strange, short, balding guy kneeling in front of her husband holding his legs up. "Uh, Jake, what's going on?" she asked.

Jake replied, "This guy is a minister. He's praying for my leg to grow out." Judging from the look on her face, she thought we were both crazy.

I invited her to come over and watch what God was about to do. I commanded his leg to grow in the name of Jesus. Instantly, his leg began to extend until it was the exact length of the other. As his leg grew, his wife gasped. "Oh my God! What just happened?" Jake was beside himself.

He stood up and began bending his leg. "The pain is gone! It's all gone! I can bend my leg! I couldn't do this!" As he walked around the parking lot, both he and his wife were crying. He then looked at his wife and said, "Donna, let him pray for your back!" I prayed for her and God healed her as well! At this point, I shared the gospel with them. Jake was overwhelmed not only by his healing but also by the message of the cross. He didn't tell me much, but from what he did tell me it sounded like God was orchestrating events to draw him to Himself. They did not receive Christ as Savior that night;

however, Jake kept saying over and over, "This is crazy, this is crazy, this is crazy! This changes everything!"

The following Sunday, I spoke at a church. Many times, I will open my message by sharing my latest God encounter story. I began to recount sitting in my car and hearing "November Rain" playing on Jake's radio. I then did the unthinkable. I began to sing the opening lines of, "November Rain" to reenact the story. I even did a little dance to go with it. It was totally unplanned. As I'm up there jamming, the thought that was going through my mind was, "I am totally the first minister in the history of the world to include a Guns 'n Roses song in his message. I hope they don't run me out of here!"

I preached my message and then invited the church to come forward for healing prayer. A woman approached me with a baby in her arms. She told me that her grandson was born with a hole in his heart and required surgery. I laid hands on him, prayed, and that was that. Later that evening, I received a call from a friend who was at the service. She was friends with the grandmother of the baby and had invited her. She then began to give me the low down of exactly what transpired earlier that day. She told me that her friend had a Catholic background and really did not know a whole lot about the things of God. She picked her grandson up that morning, and as she drove to the service she was listening to the radio. Her friend had been worried sick over her grandson's condition and the thought of him having such risky surgery.

She was thinking about the healing service that she was about to attend and decided to fleece the Lord. She said "Lord, if the song "November Rain" comes on, then I know that my grandson will be okay." "November Rain" did not come on the radio. God decided to take it to the next level! He had the minister sing it to her! At once, peace flooded her heart concerning her grandson. I was up there trying to be funny. God was using the events from the other night to pound a revelation of who He is, His nearness, and His love for her into her heart!

Over the last 21 years of stepping out, I have found that Psalm 37:23 is truth. "The steps of a man are established by the Lord, when he delights in his way." I have come to realize that this world is like a chess game, and we are the pieces. We are in the hand of the Father. He is strategizing and positioning us exactly where He wants us. He is orchestrating events to get us where we need to be. There have been many times that wrong turns, late-night grocery store runs, and other inconveniences, have actually been God set-ups. I have found that God is more than happy to disrupt my plans to get me in front of the people whom He has been drawing. When He has done that, I am always glad He did!

I laugh now as I think about the night when I met "November Rain Jake". I was completely lost and annoyed! Looking back, I now realize that I was not at all lost. I was right where God wanted me to be. I had no idea that my pulling into that convenience store was about to set off a chain of events that had eternal ramifications. The more we live on a mission for God, it becomes very clear that God is far more involved with our day-to-day lives than we thought. I have experienced so many God set-ups, that when I get inconvenienced, I now say, "Okay God, who am I here for?"

Chapter 5

Last Words

Years ago, I was looking for a partner to do street ministry with. I asked a friend from church if he'd be willing to go out with me. His reply was, "I don't think so, Kev. You're a 'catch the fish' kind of guy, and I'm more of a 'clean the fish' kind of guy." Unfortunately, this is the mindset for the majority in the church; however, we are not one or the other. We are called to be both. We are commanded to make disciples. That means we are to catch the fish and then clean our catch. There are many that believe that because you are on the introverted side that you get an evangelistic pass. Here is the hard truth. The fact that you are not comfortable with the great commission does not make you exempt from it. The reality is that this is not the call of a select few, but a command given to the entire church. Introverts and extroverts and everyone in between has been commissioned to give Jesus away. This is what makes the Great Commission great!

"And Jesus came and said to them, 'All authority in heaven and on earth has been given to me. Go therefore and make disciples of all nations, baptizing them in the name of the Father and of the Son and of the Holy Spirit, teaching them to observe all that I have commanded you. And behold, I am with you always, to the end of the age'" (Matthew 28:18-20).

When Jesus spoke these words, He was giving the church her marching orders. This was not "The Great Suggestion!" Jesus did not say, "Go and tell someone about me if they bring it up or you're feeling led to do so." Jesus said, "Go!"

This was not only a commission for fivefold evangelists. When Jesus spoke these words, He set every believer that was and ever will be into an evangelistic ministry. It was here that Jesus placed upon the entire church the authority to be His representatives on the earth. The very moment a person is born again, they receive the highest honor and greatest call. They receive the call to be an Ambassador of Christ.

All this is from God, who through Christ reconciled us to himself and gave us the ministry of reconciliation; that is, in Christ, God was reconciling the world to himself, not counting their trespasses against them, and entrusting to us the message of reconciliation. Therefore, we are ambassadors for Christ, God making his appeal through us. We implore you on behalf of Christ, be reconciled to God" (2 Corinthians 5:18-20).

My Uncle Wayne was one of my best friends. My uncle had given his life to Christ years earlier but was hurt in the church and walked away from

God. I remember the day that I found out that he had lung cancer and was in the hospital. When I heard he had cancer, I began to make plans to go to New York to see him. I told my wife that I was planning to go in a couple of weeks. She told me that she felt that I should go as soon as possible. I had figured that he was just diagnosed and that I had time. However, I listened to my wife and left the next day. When I arrived, I realized that he was in much worse shape than I thought. While I was there, the doctor came in and broke the news to him that he was dying. This was the last time that I was going to see my uncle.

I shared the gospel with him, assuring him that the Father was more than willing to take him back. I led my uncle in a prayer to recommit his life to Christ. Immediately, his countenance changed; he was at peace. I prayed for his healing; however, there was no change in his condition. He told me that he was ready to go. It was getting late, and I had to get back on the road. Before I left, my uncle took my hand and took our remaining time together to tell me everything I meant to him. Together we cried, I hugged him and kissed him goodbye, and left. The next day the cancer really began to grip my uncle. He spent his last days in a drug-induced sleep. Shortly after our visit, my uncle Wayne went to be with Jesus.

My uncle's last words to me were the nearest and dearest to his heart. He used his final words to tell me how much he loved me. They were his last words to me because they were the most important words for me to hear; the words that he did not want me to forget. The great commission was a Great Commission because these were the last words Jesus spoke to His disciples before ascending to the Father. These were the words that were nearest and dearest to the heart of Jesus. The Great Commission was the whole reason why Christ came.

Chapter 6

The Church in the Plastic Bubble

"For everyone who calls on the name of the Lord will be saved. How then will they call on him in whom they have not believed? And how are they to believe in him of whom they have never heard? And how are they to hear without someone preaching?" (Romans 10:13-14).

Jesus lived on this earth very purposely. Everything He did was done from the perspective of eternity. The goal of every believer should be to develop Christlikeness. This means we should strive to act as He acts and talk as He talks. Though many individuals do well in this, one of the biggest things that the church sadly lacks is an eternal perspective. Jesus came to earth to establish the church. Before Christ ascended to the Father, He gave the church the task of growing it. Through the Great Commission, Christ has passed us the torch and commanded us to run with it. The question is, will you run with it or choose to sit? Whichever way you answer this question, there will be personal, generational, and eternal results.

Years ago, I remember watching a movie called, "The Boy in the Plastic Bubble". John Travolta played a kid who had an issue with his immune system. His compromised immune system caused him to be extremely susceptible to sickness if he breathed normal air. The only way he could survive was by living in a plastic bubble in which he breathed purified air. Sadly, we have become the church in the plastic bubble.

When we are born again, many things begin to change. Our friends change, where we hang out changes. What we watch, what we listen to, and the things we do change. We get into the church, we start hanging out with churchy people, doing churchy things. We live in our Christian bubbles and become disconnected from the world. We know that the world is broken, but we fail to see the extent to which it is broken.

I remember years ago ministering on the streets of Poughkeepsie, NY. There was a prostitute named Karen who wanted nothing to do with me. Every time I saw her, I would attempt to talk to her, but she would ignore me. One night I was surprised when she sought me out to talk to me. Karen's forehead had a large cut on it, her nose looked broken, and her eyes were black. I asked her what happened to her. She told me that the night before, a man picked her up and brought her behind the high school. There, waiting for them, were two of his friends. She told me that they beat her and then the three of them raped her repeatedly.

She then shared with me how she came to be a prostitute. Years earlier, her young daughter had been murdered. To cope, she turned to drugs. Then she turned to harder drugs. Before long, she began selling herself to pay for her crack addiction. With tears in her eyes, she told me that she was afraid that she was going to die. I began to share the love of Jesus with her, and that He is her only hope. I explained repentance, the cross, and forgiveness. I asked her if she would like to make Him her savior. She said she would.

I began to lead her in a prayer to receive Jesus. When we got to the part where she was to ask God to forgive her, she paused. She began to cry. "I can't ask for that, I have done so many horrible things," she said. I tried again to explain God's mercy, but she refused it. As I tried to convince her that God would forgive her, a car pulled up. It was one of her "clients". She then told me that she had to go. I begged her to not go. She hugged me, kissed me on the cheek, got up, and got in the car. Just before she got in the car she turned back and looked at me. It was a hopeless look. It was a broken look. She turned, got in the car, and sped away. I saw Karen one more time, and that was the last time I saw her.

Another time I was at a convenience store pumping my gas when a car pulled up to the pump beside me. A young girl got out of the car and went inside. I began to feel as though I should go speak to her. I went inside and waited for her to finish paying for her drink. As she passed by, I said, "Excuse me. I hope you don't think this is strange, but I saw you pull up and really felt that I should come in here to pray for you." Immediately, her eyes filled with tears.

She said, "Of all days." I asked why she said that. She told me that she was going to kill herself. She (Amy) then told me that three years ago she was a cheerleader. She was the one that they threw up in the air and then would catch.

Unfortunately, they dropped her. She landed on her back and three of her discs exploded. She told me that she was prescribed pain medication. After so long, it lost its effectiveness, causing her to seek out more potent drugs. She said, "I now have two choices. I can live in constant severe pain or be an addict. I choose to be an addict. I can't do this anymore."

When I first saw Amy, I would have never thought she was in that much pain, nor a heroin addict. She looked like your typical college-aged kid. She was pretty and well-dressed. She looked healthy and happy. I felt the gift of faith rise in me. I told her, "Amy, if you let me pray for you, I think God will heal you." We went outside, and I took her hand and began to lead her in a prayer. "In the name of Jesus, I renounce the spirit of trauma, the spirit of pain, the spirit of affliction, the spirit of infirmity. I break your hold off me, and I cancel your assignment against me." She repeated after me, and then I began to command them to leave her. As I began to tell them to leave, she began to shake and cough as they came out of her. I then commanded her discs to be healed. She began to cry as she began to feel her spine moving and the pain quickly dropping! When I finished praying, the severe pain was completely gone!

I told her that God wanted to deliver her from addiction, but the foundation of freedom and the ability to remain free begins with a relationship with Jesus. I shared the gospel with her and asked if she would like to receive Jesus as her Savior. I then led her in a prayer to receive Christ. I led her through prayers renouncing spirits that drive addiction. I then commanded them to come out of her. One by one they came out with a cough. Finally, I prayed for her to receive the baptism of the Holy Spirit. Without me telling her what to expect, tongues began flowing out of her! When we parted ways, Amy felt brand new in every way.

Finally, one day I was sitting in the parking lot of Subway eating lunch. A girl got out of her car and went into the restaurant. I felt God prompting me to pray for her. I questioned whether this was God because she looked to be in perfect health. When she came out of the restaurant, I wiped the chipotle sauce off my lip, told doubt to shut up, and got out of my car. I approached her and introduced myself. I said, "This may sound crazy, but when I saw you get out of your car, I felt like God spoke to me and told me to pray for you for healing." She then told me that she had ovarian, breast, and liver cancer.

I asked if she minded if I prayed for her. She said, "Absolutely not!" I took her by the hand and invited the Holy Spirit to come and destroy the tumors in her body. Immediately she felt the power of God. She began to both laugh and cry as she felt a strong feeling of electricity in the places in her body where there were tumors! Before prayer, she had been in a great deal of pain. When we were done praying, she had no pain at all! I shared the gospel with her, and she excitedly received Christ as her Savior!

These are only three stories of extreme brokenness out of a thousand I could tell. Over the last 21 years of daily ministry to random people, I have concluded that these stories are not the exception, but they are the rule. Sin has decimated the world. Though most paint a smile on their face and look happy, healthy, and like they are keeping it all together, the pain lies just a millimeter below the surface. So many are abused, rejected, addicted, broken, and in bondage. Yet, we the church remain in our comfortable confines, unable to see what is truly going on in the world through our stained-glass windows.

It is great that we gather to pray for the lost. Obviously, prayer does much to weaken the enemies' hold, but we have all been called to the ministry of reconciling the lost back to the Father. It is not enough for us to just pray. We must put legs to those prayers. You have been called out of the sterile confines of the church to get into the mud where the broken, abused, traumatized, addicted, and dysfunctional are.

These are the people that Jesus came to save. These are the people that we were, but no longer are, because someone got in the mud with us to drag us out.

When you were born again, you received the mandate to pay it forward! For many churches, the only evangelism that is encouraged is what we do on Christmas and Easter. Praise God that people are being saved in our services, but the biblical model is that we go out into the highways and byways winning the lost and bringing them in to be discipled. I believe that church should be the place where the least amount of people are coming to Christ. This may ruffle some feathers, but we need to understand that most prostitutes, pimps, addicts, Satanists, etc., will not be coming to our Christmas and Easter extravaganzas. Ray Comfort, a great evangelist, once said, "We have as much chance of sinners wandering into our services, as we have for criminals wandering into a police station!"

Jesus didn't hole up in the temple waiting for sinners to come to Him. Jesus went to Matthew the tax collector's house because that's where the sinners were. Jesus was in the streets, hanging out with street people. Jesus spent time with people who were broken and in sin. He loved prostitutes, thieves, and addicts. He touched lepers, those who were unclean, those whom many of us in the church now shake our fists at and rail against! Jesus left the sterile confines of heaven to get into the mud with us to drag us out and clean us up.

"Or do you not know that the unrighteous will not inherit the kingdom of God? Do not be deceived: neither the sexually immoral, nor idolaters, nor adulterers, nor men who practice homosexuality, nor thieves, nor the greedy, nor drunkards, nor revilers, nor swindlers will inherit the kingdom of God. And such were some of you. But you were washed, you were sanctified, you were justified In the name of the Lord Jesus Christ and by the Spirit of our God" (1 Corinthians 6:9-11).

Jesus has commissioned all of us to come out of the plastic bubble of the church. He is sending us back into the mud where we find the hurting, the stuck, and the broken. I will close this chapter with this: it is plain to see that the United States is not on a moral decline, it is on a moral free fall. This free fall is a direct result of the brokenness in people's hearts, caused by sin. The gospel of Jesus Christ is the only hope for the world. Complaining about the moral downward spiral will never change the trajectory of the nation, nor will voting for a particular political candidate. The ONLY way to truly effective change is to share the gospel. Change will come one heart at a time as we answer the call to get in the mud to drag others out.

Chapter 7

Wired
for Evangelism

God has wired me in such a way where I can make conversation with anyone. I am comfortable approaching people whom I don't know, striking up a conversation, and keeping the conversation going. This is the way that I am wired, making me a natural for street ministry. Eventually, God began to open some doors for me to begin teaching others evangelism. The problem was that I would basically teach that my way of doing evangelism was the only way. Just about every teaching on evangelism that I have ever heard was geared for people wired similarly to me. You approach a stranger, strike up a conversation, share your testimony, share the gospel, then pray a sinner's prayer with them. This was what I was taught, so this is what I would teach. I realize now that it implies that if you are not comfortable approaching strangers, then you are ashamed of the gospel. I taught this, not realizing that the only ones who were being lit up for evangelism were people wired like I was wired, and they were already doing it!

This teaching only served to repel most people from sharing their faith. However, there were some who were guilted into it. These people would force themselves to join us for street ministry. They would look like a deer caught in headlights. These people would follow me around, totally terrified and hating every second of it. They would punch their evangelistic timecard, and never do it again. There were a few that were consistent, but many were one-hit wonders. This really bothered me, so I would guilt people harder.

My wife was a perfect example of this. My wife and I are as opposite as opposite can get. Where I am extremely outgoing, she is extremely introverted. People would approach her and say things like, "being married to Kevin, you must really love evangelism." She would nervously smile and give a fake, "Yeah, I love it."

Amy decided that she was going to push past her fear and force herself to do street ministry with me. All night long, Amy was chasing after me as I was running across the street to catch up with people. I was shouting to people to get their attention. When I would approach people, she looked terrified, and as we talked, she just stood there silent. As I think back to those few nights, that was as far out of Amy's comfort zone as she could get!

After a couple of times doing street ministry, Amy announced to me, "I hate doing street ministry, and I'm never doing it again!" A shot of fear went through me as I thought, "Oh dear God! I married someone who is ashamed of the gospel!" Meanwhile, Amy had a blog that reached women all over the world. Amy was leading these women to Jesus over the phone, via email, and in counseling sessions. This sounds ridiculous to say, but for me, this didn't count because it didn't fit in my little box of what evangelism should look like.

A few years later, Amy was studying to become a Christian counselor. One day she called me into the living room to tell me about what she was learning. She sat me down and picked up her textbook to read to me. I thought, "Oh great. She's going to read to me out of her book." I had no idea that the Holy Spirit was sitting me down to transform how I present evangelism to the church! Amy began to read to me about the different temperaments.

What really stuck out to me was the *sanguine* and the *melancholy* temperaments. Sanguines are very outgoing, and most of the time the life of the party. The more people, the better. The more people, the more charged up they get. They are great at small talk, and they connect with people on a surface level. Then, you have the melancholy temperament, which is the complete opposite. A person with a melancholy temperament is more introverted. They get drained by large crowds and need quiet to recharge. They do not do well at small talk and typically speak only when they have something to say. Melancholy people connect with others on deep levels. This is important in counseling because understanding how people are wired is key to effectively counseling them. Counseling a sanguine and a melancholy requires two completely different approaches.

As Amy shared this with me, the Holy Spirit began to show me that when it comes to teaching evangelism, I had been trying to fit round pegs in square holes! I had been teaching evangelism as a one-size-fits-all. I had an epiphany: "Not everyone is me! Not everyone is wired to do evangelism the way that I do it." My approach now is to help everyone find their place in the Great Commission. The Great Commission was given to the whole church; however, people are like snowflakes. No two are the same. Therefore, how we fulfill this commission will look differently depending on how we are wired.

Maybe you have sat under teaching like what I described above. You forced yourself to try street ministry. You hated every second of it and then felt guilty for hating it. The enemy then pours on the condemnation by reminding you of verses like, *"So everyone who acknowledges me before men, I also will acknowledge before my Father who is in heaven, but whoever denies me before men, I also will deny before my Father who is in heaven" (Matthew 10:32-33).*

You feel terrible about how un-evangelistic you are. Yet somehow you forget about the three people that you invited to the church picnic, who heard the gospel and came to Christ. Or what about the friend who was in crisis, who you met with and gave them small dose of Jesus, who eventually prayed to receive Christ? We have put such an emphasis on powerful testimonies. We love the stories of dramatic healings and deliverances, where people give their lives to Christ. Did you know that the Father throws just as big of a party in heaven when a person quietly gives their life to Him in a coffee shop as he does when someone gets healed, delivered, and then born again? In eternity, it will not matter how they came to Christ. All that will matter is that they did!

I now want to talk about the three primary ways that we can fulfill the Great Commission.

Friendship Evangelism

The first of these three what is known as friendship evangelism. Friendship evangelism is befriending someone, building a relationship, to eventually lead them to Jesus. Jesus practiced friendship evangelism at Matthew's party. "And as Jesus reclined at table in the house, behold, many tax collectors and sinners came and were reclining with Jesus and his disciples. And when the Pharisees saw this, they said to his disciples, *'Why does your teacher eat with tax collectors and sinners?' But when he heard it, he said, 'Those who are well have no need of a physician, but those who are sick. Go and learn what this means: "I desire mercy, and not sacrifice." For I came not to call the righteous, but sinners'"* (Matthew 9:10-13).

Years ago, I had a friend named Denise who would join me when I would do street ministry. Denise would join me on the streets because she did not want me going alone for fear that I'd be mugged. She was never comfortable doing street evangelism. She would often get down on herself because she really didn't want to do it and felt uncomfortable and awkward. However, Denise had an amazing ability to befriend and minister to broken women.

She would watch their children and take them to doctors' appointments. She was constantly putting herself out there for these women. They would cry on her shoulder, and she would give them doses of Jesus. More times than not, she would lead them into a relationship with Jesus.

While Denise was awkward in street evangelism, she was a master at friendship evangelism. To truly be effective at friendship evangelism, you must be willing to put yourself out there. Many times, the fruit of friendship evangelism is slow-growing. Like Christ, you must be willing to see past who a person is and see who they will be.

The best example of this is Jesus' time spent with His disciples. Throughout the time that they walked with Him, their flaws were on full display. Despite their flaws, Jesus saw who they were becoming. He knew how His influence would transform them. Jesus never gave up on them.

Invitational Evangelism

The next way we evangelize is through invitational evangelism. Invitational evangelism is simply inviting unbelievers to the place where the Savior is. You are doing evangelism when you invite people to church, small groups, or church events, where they will hear the gospel. When we invite people to where Jesus is, we are leading people to Jesus! A great biblical example of this is the woman at the well. After Jesus approached the woman at the well and read her mail concerning her five husbands, she went back to her hometown, inviting everyone to come and meet Jesus for themselves.

"'Come, see a man who told me all that I ever did. Can this be the Christ?' They went out of the town and were coming to him" (John 4:29-30). After encountering Jesus, many believed. They invited Jesus to come to Samaria where many more encountered Him and believed. Revival broke out in Samaria because one woman

invited people to the place where the Savior was.

Confrontational Evangelism

The last method of evangelism I will discuss is confrontational evangelism. Confrontational evangelism is confronting people with the gospel. Please know that confrontational evangelism should never be confrontational. I have found that the best way to engage someone is to approach them conversationally. I will begin my approach twenty feet away from them. This is important because no one likes to be pounced on. A person's split-second first impression of you is the deciding factor on whether or not someone will hear the gospel. We must tread delicately when approaching someone. When I approach people to minister to them, very seldom do I start blasting them with Jesus. When we bombard people with Jesus, many times they will say, "No thanks," and move on because of their misconceptions of Christians.

Most times I will look for something on the person to strike up a conversation with them, such as tattoos, t-shirts, animals, whatever stands out to me. I start the conversation by asking them questions. This is a great method because what I have found is people love to talk about themselves. If a person has a tattoo, I'll ask what it means. If a person is wearing a shirt with a rock band or sports team on it, I'll ask questions about their shirt. The purpose of the questions is to start a conversation. As I ask questions, I listen and ask more questions about their answers.

As we have a conversation, we are both becoming comfortable with one another. At a point in the conversation, I'll say, "Hey, I'm a Christian. Is there anything I can pray for you for?" Most times they will tell you about a family member that is sick or having some other difficulty. I will pray for that person and then ask,

"What can I pray for *you* for?" Most times they will share their needs, and at this point, we have moved into a gospel conversation.

A few years back, while doing street ministry, I approached a guy and asked if I could pray for him. He laughed and said, "No thanks." I noticed he had a Star Wars shirt on. I asked him if he had seen the new Star Wars movie, to which he said he had. I then asked him his opinion of it. He and I then had a twenty-minute conversation about Star Wars. When I knew he was more comfortable with me, I told him that I was on the streets praying for people. I asked him again if I could pray for him. This time he said yes! He told me that was separated from his wife due to marital issues. He was missing his wife and children, so he asked me to pray for his situation.

At that point, I began to share the gospel with him and apply it to his situation. I told him that the first step to repairing what was broken in his family was to allow God to fix what is broken in his heart. I prayed with him to receive Christ and prayed with him for the restoration of his family. That night, Jesus touched him powerfully!

Chapter 8

What is Success?

I have found that most people measure success in evangelism by how many people they get to parrot a sinner's prayer after them, or if the person they ministered to shows up for church on Sunday morning. There was a time in my life when I believed this as well. I would go out on the street, preach my little heart out and lead people in sinner's prayers. On Sunday morning, my eyes would be fixed on the door of the church, waiting for them to swing open and see my prize walk through the door. Halfway into the second song in worship, my heart would begin to sink as I began to realize that they were not going to show. I was becoming incredibly frustrated. I was working my butt off but seeing no fruit. I began to question whether not I was anointed for evangelism. I wanted to quit.

One night, we went out on the street and seemingly hit brick wall after brick wall. I shared the gospel with a few people, but it was quite uneventful. We were in an area of the city that was known for prostitution and drug deals. That is where I ran into Samantha. I knew her from my childhood. Her grandmother had lived across the street from us. I hadn't seen her in years.

What I remembered the most about Samantha was her eyes. Her eyes were like blue crystals. However, when I ran into Samantha that night on the street, I was struck by how black and lifeless her eyes were. I said to her, "I don't know what you're into, but I know that God loves you and can set you free from whatever is holding you captive." I gave her a tract, she thanked me, and quickly left. That evening we returned to the church. My pastor asked how we made out. I replied, "Terrible! No one prayed to receive Christ!" I drove home that night feeling very discouraged.

Three months later, I pulled into my father's driveway and got out of my truck. As I was about to go inside, someone shouted my name. I turned to find Samantha running towards me! I will never forget her eyes. They were deep blue, seemingly dancing, and very much alive! She threw her arms around me and thanked me for what I had done for her. I wasn't sure what she was talking about. She told me that the night I ran into her, that she was on her way to buy cocaine. She told me that she felt incredible conviction as I said what I said to her. She just wanted to get away from me. She told me that when she was out of my view, she sat on a stoop and began to read the tract I had given her. After reading it, she couldn't buy cocaine. She went home.

The next morning, she checked herself into a drug rehab. A few days later, she attended a Bible study where a little old lady led her to Jesus! She said that day she was completely delivered from all desire to use drugs. In the months that followed, both Samantha's immediate and extended family began to follow Jesus. This was the result of my bad night on the street where I hit brick wall after brick wall.

God used Samantha to completely change my perception of what success in evangelism looks like. I have come to realize that any time a person hears the message of the cross of Christ, it is a success. The gospel message is the kindness of God on display, and it is God's kindness that leads men to repentance.

"Or do you presume on the riches of his kindness and forbearance and patience, not knowing that God's kindness is meant to lead you to repentance?" (Romans 2:4).

Our job is to plant the seed of the gospel and

water seeds that have been sown, but it is God's job to cause it to grow.

"I planted, Apollos watered, but God gave the growth. So neither he who plants nor he who waters is anything, but only God who gives the growth" (1 Corinthians 3:6-7).

Years ago, my family and I were at Pizza Hut. When my kids were younger, without fail, every time we were seated in a restaurant, they would immediately have to use the bathroom. So here I am waiting for my kids to do their business. While waiting, I decided to be about my Father's business.

There was a guy who looked to be in his early thirties waiting for his food. I introduced myself to him and asked if there was anything that I could pray for him for? He couldn't think of anything. I then told him that God loved him and that He died for him so he could be made brand new. At that point, his food was ready. As he walked out, he thanked me for saying what I said to him. I gave him my ministry card and he left.

Six months later, he called me. He introduced himself as the guy I spoke with in Pizza Hut. He sounded agitated. He asked me why I talked to him that day. I told him that it wasn't by chance that we had our conversation, but it was a God set-up. He then told me that he has not been able to get my words out of his head. As he spoke, he became increasingly angry. He then said, "I want God, but I don't want God! I don't know what I want!"

I told him, "God is after your heart, but there is a very real devil who wants your heart as well." There was a war for his heart taking place! I told him, "If you want to experience peace, give your whole heart over to Jesus."

He replied, "I don't know what I want! I don't even know why I called you!" At that point, he hung up.

As I thought back to our conversation, I was struck by the simplicity of it. "God loves you, God died for you." Seven simple words that for him were not the least bit simple. Those seven words were jackhammering through the hardness of his heart. I never spoke with him again, but I fully expect to meet him again in heaven.

We the church have made evangelism so much more difficult than it needs to be. When it comes to evangelism, many of us have been taught different presentations or formulas to engage the lost. We have had teachings and are told, "This is how it should be done." Many have been intimidated under the assumption that we must preach a five-point sermon to someone and have them parrot a sinner's prayer. Anything less than this is not evangelism. I am not writing this book to give you the 'latest and greatest, never fail, never get persecuted'- style of evangelism. I don't have a formula or a presentation.

If you desire to see the Kingdom of God advance, if you want to be successful in evangelism, then do or say *something*. Simply open your mouth. Tell someone that Jesus loves them and ask someone if you can pray for them. God can and does do so much with words or actions that we perceive as being insignificant. People are lost, broken, and without hope. They are watching, listening, and being affected by you more than they'll let on. As you decide to make this your lifestyle, your confidence will increase, and you will get opportunities to share on deeper levels. For those who dedicate their lives to scattering seed everywhere they go, their lives will be marked by abundant fruit. Those who live their life to scatter seed will see great success in evangelism.

Chapter 9

The Garden

"Then he said to his disciples, 'The harvest is plentiful, but the laborers are few; therefore, pray earnestly to the Lord of the harvest to send out laborers into his harvest'" (Matthew 9:37:38).

The first time I met Randy, the date was 9/12/2001. It was the day after the Twin Towers fell. I approached Randy and started to talk to him about the tragedy. I shared how none of those people expected to die, and how our next breath is not guaranteed. I began to tell him about Jesus. In a swear-filled rant, Randy told me that he did not know any of those people, or care about them. He then told me that if I did not get away from him, that he was going to kill me. Judging by the look in his eyes, he meant it. I heeded Randy's warning and moved on.

Some might say that this encounter with Randy was a colossal failure. I say it was a raging success! In the previous chapter I made the seemingly crazy statement that when it comes to sharing Christ, there is no such this as failure. Let me explain.

For the last several years, I've had a garden. I did not grab a handful of seeds, go to my backyard, find a spot, and throw the seed on the ground and say, "See you in the fall!" It would be crazy to think that anything would grow that way! I went out to my backyard and selected the spot where I would plant the seeds. Unfortunately, when I initially dug my garden, I did not have a rototiller. I dug my garden by hand with a pickaxe. When I first began the digging process, I would swing the pickaxe towards the earth; however, the hard soil revolted against the tool. I was determined, so I continued to drive the tool into the earth. After much hard work, the soil was ready for seeds. After the seeds were planted, I would come out and water the garden daily. Soon, tiny plants began to emerge from the soil. Eventually, I was harvesting vegetables.

The process of someone coming into relationship with Christ is very much like planting a garden. After enough encounters with the love of Jesus, a person's heart will begin to soften and be made ready for the seed of the gospel to be planted. As others come along and water this seed, it begins to take root, leading to an eventual harvest.

Every person that comes to Christ goes through this process. Sometimes we are the one with the pickaxe. Sometimes we are the one with the watering can. Praise God, sometimes we get to be the one with the basket that God sends to harvest what He has grown. To have the harvest, there must first be the breaking up of the hard ground of the heart. Many times, the rejection we experience is a reaction to the love of Christ breaking up this hard soil. To have the end of the process, there must be a beginning. Therefore, anytime we participate in someone's process, whether their reaction to us is negative or not, we are successful!

After my initial run-in with Randy, I began to see him quite a bit. I realized that Randy was homeless. When I would see him, I would ask if I could pray for him or simply tell him that Jesus loves him. Most of the time, he would swear at me, telling me to leave him alone. I was relentless!

One night, I was driving down Main Street and saw him sitting on a bench. My mother had given me a plate of food, and I felt the Lord telling me to give it to him. I pulled over and approached him. I gave him the food and told him that Jesus loved him. Randy took the food and thanked me. I was amazed, this was our first interaction where he wasn't cussing me out! He didn't swear at me, but I could tell he wasn't ready to talk. I left praising God for beginning to soften Randy's heart.

I saw Randy a few weeks later. Randy was huddled up in a doorway trying to keep warm. I drove to my mother's house and raided her closet for a couple of blankets. I then drove back to the place where Randy was. Randy was sitting up and saw me coming with the blankets. As I approached him, Randy asked me, "What is up with you? I've treated you so badly, but you keep coming back. Why would you do these things for me?" At that point, I shared with him how Jesus kept pursuing me, though I'd continuously spit in his face.

I told him, "It is the Jesus in me that is in pursuit of you." I began to share the gospel with him. As I spoke, tears began to pour out of his eyes. When I was done, I led Randy to Christ. Immediately, the rage was gone from his eyes, and his entire countenance changed, the darkness was gone. When we share the gospel and demonstrate Christ, it is impossible to fail.

Chapter 10

Takeaways
From the
Pride Parade

few years back, my wife, myself, and a
small group of others were ministering at
the Pittsburgh Gay Pride parade. It had
begun to lightly rain, so Amy and I went under
an overhang to get out of the rain. While we
were waiting out the rain, a guy joined us under
the overhang. This guy was decked out in
leather: leather hat, leather belt, no shirt, a
leather choker around his neck, with a leather

strap that connected from the choker to his belt. To accessorize his outfit, he had his nipples pierced with two huge hoop nipple rings. Looking at this guy, I was trying to figure out what angle I would take to strike up a conversation with him. I went with the obvious. Pointing at his nipples, I said, "Man, those babies must have killed your nipples!"

He replied, "Yeah, especially the second time around." He then told me that he had gotten his nipples pierced and then tore his ACL before his nipples could heal. He had to have surgery and could not have metal in his body. He took them out and his nipple holes closed up.

The second time he got them pierced, there was scar tissue. He then proceeded to tell me in detail about his and his boyfriend's sex life and how that involves the nipple rings. I kind of wanted to cry. However, I didn't tell him to stop. I didn't have any kind of look on my face; I just listened. As he spoke, despite the topic of conversation, God was showing me that this man had scoliosis, so I asked if he did. Amazed, he said he did and asked me how I knew. I told him that God told me, and that God wanted to heal him. He was happy to let me pray for him. I led him in a prayer to renounce scoliosis. I commanded it out of him. He felt it climb his spine to the base of his skull and then come out of him. I then placed my hand on his back and commanded his spine to straighten. Immediately, I could feel his spine move under my hand. In moments, his spine was straight, and all his pain was gone. He bent over and touched his toes for the first time in years.

I then began to share the love of God with him. He told me that He was raised in a church, and that his family were all believers. He then told me that he had confessed to his church that he was attracted to the same sex, and although he had never acted on his attraction, he was driven out of the church. Feeling rejected by God, he entered a gay lifestyle. I told him that Jesus is faithful to him. I explained to him that Jesus died on the cross for him; that the blood of Jesus was shed for him so his sins could be forgiven. I told him that Jesus came for him, that He healed him to get his attention. I said, "The goal of this is not for you to join a religion or a church, but first things first: Jesus wants a relationship with you." He said, "But I'm gay. I can't change that."

I told him, "You're right, you can't change that! But what you can do is turn to Jesus. If you follow Him with your whole heart, with a desire to turn from your sin, He'll make you into exactly who He created you to be." At the end of the conversation, I asked if he would like to receive Christ as Savior. He said he was not yet there. I didn't try to push him. I knew that God was working in him. Before we parted ways, he told me that I was unlike any Christian he had ever met, and that he had a lot to think about.

There are many key takeaways from this encounter:

Have a conversation with people to lead them to a place of comfort. When I approached him, I didn't just blast him with the gospel. Because of false perceptions concerning Christianity, many people do not respond well to the blasting approach. By striking up a conversation about his nipple rings, he was put at ease with me, which eventually led to me being able to share truth with him.

I could have made a disgusted face and rebuked him for talking about his sex life like he did. All that would have done was put him on the defensive and cut all lines of life-giving communication. Over the past twenty-one years, I have ministered to people who were smoking marijuana, shooting heroin, drinking, swearing, even making drug deals in the middle of our conversation. Keep in mind: when we share Christ, we must be willing to meet people where they are at, to bring them to where we are. Romans 5:8 tells us that while we were actively in our sin, Christ died for us. When Christ came for us, He didn't come pointing a boney religious finger at our chest. He came in love, and His love drew us in. His love led us to repent of our sin.

There are many who believe that if God is real, He is angry and far from them because of their sin. A tangible encounter with God will open anyone's eyes to the reality, nearness, and love of the Father. If God was angry with a person, He wouldn't heal that person. To experience God's presence is to experience His love. A run-in with God's love changes everything!

Truth must be delivered in love. Loveless truth is like a baseball bat to the head. Love with no truth produces false converts. Truth without love repels people. The word repentance is not a dirty word to sinners if we effectively demonstrate the love of the Savior Jesus, who they will turn to and follow.

We don't preach 'change and come to Christ,' but 'come to Christ, become a disciple and He'll change you!' We are powerless to change ourselves. If we could, Jesus would not have had to die. When we call people to repentance, we are calling them to choose to turn from a life of sin and follow Jesus. As a person wholeheartedly pursues Jesus, He makes straight all that is crooked.

We do not have to focus on certain sins when talking about repentance. It is all vile to God. There is not one specific sin that sends someone to hell, but a person's decision to live independent of Jesus. Refusing Christ's offer of forgiveness sends a person to hell.

Parroting a sinner's prayer does not save. Encounters with God's goodness do. This encounter was far more successful because I did not pressure him to pray a sinner's prayer. I remember the first time I gave my son medicine. I had a syringe full of Children's Tylenol. I called my son to me and said, "Daddy has candy for you." My son opened his mouth, and I squirted the entire syringe down his throat, causing him to choke. He spit it all out. I tried to give him more, but because I had given him more medicine than he was ready for, he resisted the next time I tried to give him his medicine.

The same is true when we try to force someone to pray a sinner's prayer before they are ready. If I had pressured him, he may have prayed it because he felt pressured, and then walked away feeling bullied or pushed into something he was not ready to do. This would have produced no change in his heart and closed him off from receiving from the next laborer that God would send across his path.

Chapter 11

How to Love Not Your Life Even Unto Death

A few years ago, I took a poll. I asked people what is the number one reason that prevents them from sharing the gospel. There was a wide range of answers such as, "I don't know the Bible well enough. What if I'm asked a question that I cannot answer? I feel like people do not want to be bothered." The number one answer that people gave was fear of persecution. I would love to say that persecution is not a thing. I would love to say that if you purpose to live your life on mission for God, that you will never experience rejection, but I cannot. If you are striving to live a life of holiness, if you are living to populate heaven, then inevitably you will experience persecution. For this reason, I felt it was necessary to include a chapter on persecution.

Jesus very pointedly tells us that the world hated Him, therefore it will hate us. *"If the world hates you, know that it has hated me before it hated you. If you were of the world, the world would love you as its own; but because you are not of the world, but I chose you out of the world, therefore the world hates you" (John 15:18-19).*

James 4:4 also tells us that if we are a friend of the world, that would make us an enemy of God. If we turn that around, a friend of God is an enemy of the world. There is a false American gospel that says that Jesus died on the cross to make us fat, rich, and happy. However, there are millions of on-fire believers living in persecuted countries who are not living out *that* reality. Contrary to what we have been fed, Christianity is not about living your best life now, but it is all about sowing into eternity! When we give our lives to Christ and begin to truly live for Him, your life, as far as the world is concerned, will get more difficult.

"Behold, the hour is coming, indeed it has come, when you will be scattered, each to his own home, and will leave me alone. Yet I am not alone, for the Father is with me. I have said these things to you, that in me you may have peace. In the world you will have tribulation. But take heart; I have overcome the world" (John 16:32-33).

While Jesus did not die on the cross to make our lives problem-free, He does promise to give us peace amid whatever hardships we face. This is a peace that passes understanding.

We must keep this in mind: all persecution is demonically driven. *"For we do not wrestle against flesh and blood, but against rulers, against authorities, against cosmic powers over this present darkness, against the spiritual forces of evil in the heavenly places" (Ephesians 6:12).*

Our enemy is not people. When we understand that the persecutor is being demonically driven to do so, it helps us to walk in love and not lose our witness. This understanding is what enabled Christ to pray for those who beat Him to a bloody pulp and hung Him on a cross. Christ died on the cross to deliver humanity from the yoke of the devil. It was this yoke of bondage that caused them to act out as they did. It is the same yoke that drives persecution against the gospel. For this same reason, we preach the glorious gospel of Christ! It is the anointing on the message of the gospel that breaks the yoke.

If we live on mission for God, persecutions will come. However, 1 Peter 4:14 tells us that when we are persecuted, the Spirit of God and glory rests on us. Not only does the Spirit of God and glory rest on us, but we are laying up treasures in heaven. *"Blessed are those who are persecuted for righteousness' sake, for theirs is the kingdom of heaven. Blessed are you when others revile you and persecute you and utter all kinds of evil against you falsely on my account. Rejoice and be glad, for your reward is great in heaven, for so they persecuted the prophets who were before you" (Matthew 5:10-12).*

The Apostle Paul is a great example of someone who was willing to endure persecution for the sake of the gospel. Literally, as soon as Paul was born again, the Lord began to speak to him about what He was to face. *"But the Lord said to him, "Go, for he is a chosen instrument of mine to carry my name before the Gentiles and kings and the children of Israel. For I will show him how much he must suffer for the sake of my name" (Acts 9:15-16).* Throughout the book of Acts, we read account after account of Paul suffering for the gospel.

In 2 Corinthians, Paul gives a recap of all he has endured for the sake of the gospel.

"Are they Hebrews? So am I. Are they Israelites? So am I. Are they offspring of Abraham? So am I. Are they servants of Christ? I am a better one—I am talking like a madman—with far greater labors, far more imprisonments, with countless beatings, and often near death. Five times I received at the hands of the Jews the forty lashes less one. Three times I was beaten with rods. Once I was stoned. Three times I was shipwrecked; a night and a day I was adrift at sea; on frequent journeys, in danger from rivers, danger from robbers, danger from my own people, danger from Gentiles, danger in the city, danger in the wilderness, danger at sea, danger from false brothers; in toil and hardship, through many a sleepless night, in hunger and thirst, often without food, in cold and exposure. And, apart from other things, there is the daily pressure on me of my anxiety for all the churches. Who is weak, and I am not weak? Who is made to fall, and I am not indignant?" (2 Corinthians 11:21-29).

It is easy to read this list of persecutions and gloss over it. Read it again. This time imagine what it must have felt like to endure each of these things that Paul went through. Despite these afflictions, Paul kept going. He counted his life as nothing. Paul kept an eternal perspective. He knew this life was only a blink of an eye, a breath. He had a revelation of glory.

It was this revelation that caused Paul to speak these parting words to the Ephesian elders: *"You yourselves know how I lived among you the whole time from the first day that I set foot in Asia, serving the Lord with all humility and with tears and with trials that happened to me through the plots of the Jews; how I did not shrink from declaring to you anything that was profitable, and teaching you in public and from house to house, testifying both to Jews and to Greeks of repentance toward God and of faith in our Lord Jesus Christ. "And now, behold, I am going to Jerusalem, constrained by the Spirit, not knowing what will happen to me there, except that the Holy Spirit testifies to me in every city that imprisonment and afflictions await me. But I do not account my life of any value nor as precious to myself, if only I may finish my course and the ministry that I received from the Lord Jesus, to testify to the gospel of the grace of God" (Ephesians 20:18-24).*

I remember years ago, after a meeting, a group of us went to Denny's to eat. There was a large group of teenagers there. After we ate, I walked over and attempted to strike up a conversation with them. After chatting a bit, I asked them what they believed as far as God went. The kid directly to my right spoke up. He said, "How about you stop trying to shove your God down our throats!" I put my hand on his shoulder and I told him, "I'm not shoving God down your throat."

He replied, "We don't want to hear about it. Now take your hand off my shoulder!" He knocked me back on my heels. His words stung! I looked like a fool in front of twenty teenagers, as well as the group that I came with. I wanted to lash out at him but kept quiet. I turned and left the restaurant. As I walked to my car, I could feel the burn of rejection. As I sat there thinking about what I had just experienced, the Lord spoke to me.

He said, "Are you willing to allow yourself to feel the burn of rejection if it will prevent someone from going to hell?" This is the question we all must answer. Are you willing to risk rejection; are you willing to feel uncomfortable? I have made the choice to allow myself to feel the burn of rejection. I have decided that I will risk persecution if it prevents someone from going into the fires of hell.

Years ago, when I would do evangelism seminars, my big "closer" would be a teaching on hell. I would talk about the sights, sounds, and smells of hell. I would use scripture as well as testimonies of those who I felt were reputable, who had visited or had visions of hell, to paint a picture of how awful hell is. The goal of this was to motivate people to share the gospel. It would work, well...for a while, anyway. People would run out of the church and share Jesus with everything that moved. However, after some time, the message would get fuzzy, and soon most would settle back into their safe places.

It was really frustrating to see everyone so excited to be a witness, only to watch their fire go out. I felt like I was missing something. One day I was reading Paul's account of the persecution he had suffered. I asked the Lord to show me what was *the thing that kept Paul going amid such horrible persecution. The Lord led me to my answer: "For if we are beside ourselves, it is for God; If we are in our right mind, it is for you. For the love of Christ controls us, because we have concluded this: that one has died for all, therefore all have died; and he died for all, that those who live might no longer live for themselves but for him who for their sake died and was raised" (2 Corinthians 5:13-15).*

Guilting or scaring people will do little to cause them to risk persecution, but love will do much. I have come to realize that the church does not have a boldness deficiency, but many are deficient in their understanding of the Father's love. When we come into a revelation of the Father's love for us, we fall in love with Him, but we also fall in love with what He loves. God's love working in us causes us to love people. Jesus was moved with compassion, and it is compassion that moves us. Love cannot remain idle or silent in the presence of brokenness. It was love that compelled Jesus to the cross. It is love that will cause us to love not our lives even to the death.

God, What's Wrong with Me?

Nothing will ever compare with the night that I was born again. I had lost my job and my friends. Here I was, twenty-seven years old and living with my father, and now my girlfriend of 6 years had just dumped me. She dropped me off at my house and hugged me goodbye. As I watched her back out of my driveway for the last time, my plan was to go into my house and take my life. As I watched her pull away, I muttered the name, "Jesus". I was not praying but was taking the name of the

Lord in vain. When I said his name, His presence came powerfully. I immediately fell on my face, and rivers of tears began to flow from my eyes. I was having an encounter with the goodness of God. In seeing His goodness, the true state of my heart was revealed to me. This powerful revelation produced a gut-wrenching repentance. As I lay on my face on my front lawn, I began to ask God to forgive me for running from Him. As I did, waves of love washed through my body. As His presence washed over me, I could feel things leaving me.

I now realize that I was being delivered of demons. That night, twenty-seven years of depression, anger, rejection, fear, and suicidal thoughts left me. On March 25, 2000, at 3:00 am, I encountered Jesus, and my life was radically changed.

I began going to a Dutch Reformed church. The people of this church were nice, but the Holy Spirit was not in this church. I was on fire for God. Next to the pastor, I was the big spiritual man on campus! I didn't know anything theologically, but I was passionate.

As time went by, I felt the Lord nudging me out of that church. God then placed me in a small charismatic church. Once I got around Spirit-filled believers, I began to realize that I was no longer the "big spiritual man on campus." It was becoming glaringly obvious that there was something missing in my walk with God. I would watch people in worship. They seemed so connected to God, like they were lost in His presence. Then there were others who would weep while they worshipped. By about the fourth song, I would be ready for worship to be over. I would find myself being upset with myself for feeling this way and annoyed with them because I wanted this connection in worship but could not seem to get there.

Not only did they have a passion for worship that I didn't have, but the same was true when it came to the Word of God. They seemingly had such a love for it. They talked about the revelations they were receiving, and how the Lord was speaking to them through it.

Again, I would find myself becoming angry because reading the Bible was more of a chore for me. I had a difficult time understanding it. It didn't jump off the page at me like it seemed to for others. For me, reading the Bible was drudgery. The fact that it was so difficult for me to read, it made me wonder if there was something wrong with me. And forget about prayer! After five minutes, I had pretty much said everything that I knew to say. I would then sit there frustrated because I felt like I should have so much more to say and like I should feel more connected than I did.

Then there were the special meetings when the Holy Spirit would be moving powerfully. I would sit in my seat terrified. I would watch people falling down when the Holy Spirit would touch them, and I wanted no part of that! All my friends would go forward for a "touch from God,", but I would remain glued to my seat, silently praying that the meeting would end. As we would drive home, everyone would be so excited about what God did, while I just felt relieved that it was over. As I would listen to them, I would wonder, "What do they have, that I don't have?" With that question came another question, "God, what is wrong with me?"

Finally, I went to a friend and confessed that I felt something was missing from my walk with God. That's when he shared with me about the baptism in the Holy Spirit. He told me that this experience would give me a greater passion and boldness for God, as well as the ability to pray in tongues. He also told me that it was for everyone. He took me through the scriptures, and reluctantly I allowed him to pray for me. However, when he prayed, I was so apprehensive that I couldn't receive anything. Again, I was then left wondering: "What's wrong with me?"

Not long after that, my friend invited me to a special service at his church. Midway through the worship, they gave an altar call for the baptism in the Holy Spirit. I figured I would give the speaking in tongues thing another whirl. I went forward and suddenly found myself surrounded by eight people. They instructed me to not pray in English, but to only pray in tongues. I thought to myself, "I don't know any tongue words." At this point, I was greatly regretting responding to the altar call! Next thing I knew, I had eight hands on my head, and a bunch of people yelling weird-sounding words in my face! I had to get out of there! I pushed all their hands off me, squeezed through a hole in the circle, and ran out of the church. At this point, I was good with God the Father and Jesus the Son, but I officially wanted no part of the Holy Spirit or His baptism.

In March of 2001, I was invited to a conference in Connecticut. Little did I know that this conference would be the event that would catapult me into my destiny. I had only gotten a few hours of sleep the night before. I did not want to go, but felt that God wanted me there, so I went kicking and screaming in my heart. When I got there, I was miserable. It wasn't just, "I'm tired" miserable, but it was an, "I'm angry and I need to get out of this place" kind of miserable. This anger was compounded by the fact that I was stuck there for the entire day! I realize now that this was a last-ditch effort by the enemy to try to prevent what God was about to do.

The pastor began to preach and, due to my agitation, I heard absolutely nothing. About three-quarters through the service, the Holy Spirit fell on me. Suddenly, I became overcome by emotion. I began to sob. Once again, through huge tears, the Lord began to deliver me. I could literally feel the anger leaving me as God's presence embraced me.

The pastor then gave an altar call for anyone desiring the baptism in the Holy Spirit. Without hesitation or fear, I ran down to the altar. I stood there with one hundred other hungry believers, as the pastor gave the instructions. He told us that he was going to ask Jesus to baptize us in His Spirit. He said He was going to count to three and when He got to three, the Spirit of God would fall on us, and we would be filled with the Holy Spirit and receive our prayer language.

This was the big build-up! I was ready! He began to pray, "Jesus, come and baptize them in your Holy Spirit!" At once, a word came up from my belly, and I spoke it out: "Roshunda." Immediately I thought, "Roshunda? What in the world is 'roshunda'? That's not tongues." The minister then instructed everyone to come up and briefly speak in tongues into the microphone. One after the other, they went forward. Some had one word that they spoke over and over. Others came up and spoke many words, while some sang in tongues.

As the people went forward, one after the other, my heart sank. There I stood with the handful of people of people who didn't receive. Again, I thought to myself, "God, what is wrong with me? Maybe this isn't for everyone." I felt like a Jesus reject.

The pastor then addressed those of us who were still standing there. He said, "The devil wants you to believe that you're speaking gibberish. It is not gibberish, you got it!" At that moment, faith rose up in me. I ran up to him, grabbed the microphone out of his hand, and spoke in tongues. When I opened my mouth, a flood of words thundered out of it! That day I danced, sang, and shouted. I laid on my face and wept, all in worship to the King of kings. That day, I was introduced to the Holy Spirit, and instantly fell in love with Him. I realized that He was what I had been missing.

That experience, on that day in March 2001, catapulted me into my destiny. I was empowered and emboldened for ministry! I quickly began to realize that not only does God desire to pour out His Spirit upon us, but He desires to pour out His Holy Spirit through us. The day I received the baptism in the Spirit was the day my relationship with Him became one of intimacy.

Prior to the Holy Spirit baptism, I was comfortable with God the Father and God the Son, however, I feared God the Holy Spirit. It has been my experience that this is the case for many. Sadly, many in the church do not understand the Holy Spirit's role in their Christianity.

Do you remember when you were living like a Viking, and then one day you had the thought: "This life I've been living is getting old." That was the Holy Spirit. Do you remember the first time you had the thought to begin looking into Christianity? That was the Holy Spirit. Do you remember the first time you stepped into a church and felt like the pastor was speaking directly to you? That was the Holy Spirit.

Do you remember the close of the message, how you knew you needed to respond to the altar call? Again, that was the Holy Spirit. Do you remember the feeling of joy that you left with? That was the Holy Spirit's presence on the inside of you. The Holy Spirit reveals God's Word to us. He leads us, He counsels us, guides us, He speaks to us. The Holy Spirit comforts us and convicts us. He's the one who has been pushing the buttons, pulling the levers, and turning the wheels. It is the Holy Spirit that has been working behind the scenes, making your Christianity what it is. He is all you've got! If He is all you've got, why wouldn't you want as much of Him as you can get?

.

The Church is Born

The day I received the baptism in the Holy Spirit, my Christianity was lit on fire. Not only was my passion ignited, but I began to walk in boldness and power that I had not walked in before. In the past, I had shared the gospel with people when the opportunity presented itself, but after being filled with the Holy Ghost, I began to seek people out to share the gospel! It was after this encounter that I began to go out on the streets to share the gospel on a regular basis. Although I didn't know it, my ministry had begun.

My process falls right in line with scripture. We see this first in Christ's ministry.

"Then Jesus came from Galilee to the Jordan to John, to be baptized by him. John would have prevented him, saying, 'I need to be baptized by you, and do you come to me?' But Jesus answered him, 'Let it be so now, for thus it is fitting for us to fulfill all righteousness.' Then he consented. And when Jesus was baptized, immediately he went up from the water, and behold, the heavens were opened to him, and he saw the Spirit of God descending like a dove and coming to rest on him; and behold, a voice from heaven said, *'This is my beloved Son, with whom I am well pleased'"* (Matthew 3:13-17).

Shortly after this encounter, Jesus' earthly ministry began. It was the same with the first disciples.

"On the evening of that day, the first day of the week, the doors being locked where the disciples were for fear of the Jews, Jesus came and stood

among them and said to them, 'Peace be with you.' When he had said this, he showed them his hands and his side. Then the disciples were glad when they saw the Lord. Jesus said to them again, 'Peace be with you. As the Father has sent me, even so I am sending you.' And when he had said this, he breathed on them and said to them, 'Receive the Holy Spirit'" (John 20:19-22).

When Jesus breathed on the disciples, the Holy Spirit took up residence within them, and caused their sin-dead spirits to come to life. At that point, He removed from them their sin nature and replaced it with the God nature. This was the born-again experience. After having received the Holy Spirit at conversion, in Acts 1, the disciples were told to expect a second encounter with the Holy Spirit. Jesus instructed the disciples to stay put in Jerusalem until they were endued with power.

"And while staying with them he ordered them not to depart from Jerusalem, but to wait for the promise of the Father, which, he said, 'you heard

from me; for John baptized with water, but you will be baptized with the Holy Spirit not many days from now'" (Acts 1:4-5).

A few verses down, Jesus explains that the purpose for this second encounter with the Holy Spirit is to empower them for the work of evangelism. *"But you will receive power when the Holy Spirit has come upon you, and you will be my witnesses in Jerusalem and in all Judea and Samaria, and to the end of the earth" (Acts 1:8).*

Prior to the baptism of the Spirit, these men were all about themselves, arguing about who would be the greatest in the Kingdom. Not only were they selfish, but they were full of fear, running away when Jesus was arrested and even denying they knew Him to some slave girls. They had no idea how radically their lives were about to change. *"When the day of Pentecost arrived, they were all together in one place. And suddenly there came from heaven a sound like a mighty rushing wind, and it filled the entire house where they were sitting. And divided tongues as of fire appeared to them and rested on each one of them. And they were all filled with the Holy Spirit and began to speak in other tongues as the Spirit gave them utterance" (Acts 2:1-4).*

This event was one of the most significant events in human history! The disciples were filled with the Holy Spirit and empowered for the hefty call that was on their lives. Empowered and emboldened by the Holy Spirit, they now sought to save the very ones they had been hiding from! Under the anointing of the Holy Spirit, Peter boldly preached the gospel. That day, three thousand souls were added to the Kingdom, and the church exploded into existence.

The baptism of the Holy Spirit transformed the first disciples from fearful men into powerful men of God. These men stood in the face of persecution to boldly proclaim the gospel of Jesus Christ, even to their death. Because of that encounter in the upper room, the gospel has gone around the world, and here we are today!

Chapter 14

And You Shall Receive Power

As a fivefold evangelist, I am called to win the lost, but also to equip the body for evangelistic ministry. God has anointed me to pray for other people to receive the Holy Spirit baptism. I have seen thousands of believers receive this experience, and subsequently get lit on fire to share the gospel. Years ago, I had a friend named Kerm. Kerm by vocation was a lumberjack. He was that guy who was always there to help if there was a job to do. He was the first to arrive, and the last to leave.

We belonged to a church that required set up and tear down. Kerm would, many times, have carried everything up from the basement before anyone else showed up. Kerm could build or fix anything. He was quiet and kind, a servant of servants. However, as far as ministry went, he was the last person that you would expect to minister evangelistically.

One evening, I held an altar worker training. At the time, I was the head of our prayer ministry. Kerm's wife had an interest in being on the team, so she attended, and Kerm sat in on it with his wife. At the close, I invited those who had not received the baptism of the Spirit to come forward to receive it. Kerm came forward and was baptized in the Holy Spirit. In the days that followed, I began hearing stories of Kerm going to the sawmill and laying hands on the backs of the other lumberjacks. These men were being healed. Kerm was then sharing the gospel with them, and they were getting saved! The baptism of the Holy Spirit transformed Kerm into a lumberjack evangelist!

"But you will receive power when the Holy Spirit has come upon you, and you will be my witnesses in Jerusalem and in all Judea and Samaria, and to the end of the earth" (Acts 1:8).

Many in the church have viewed speaking in tongues as the end-all, be-all evidence that a person has received the baptism of the Spirit. However, Acts 1:8 does not say "and you will receive tongues when the Holy Spirit has come upon you;" it says, "you will receive power." I one hundred percent believe that receiving the ability to pray in tongues is an evidence that you have received the Holy Spirit baptism. However, I believe that the true end-all, be-all evidence of the baptism of the Spirit is an upgrade in boldness to share the gospel, an upgrade in passion for the things of God, and the power of the Holy Spirit functioning through our lives in ministry!

It is no wonder that the devil will work so hard to put entire churches in fear of it. The devil is a jerk, but he is not a stupid jerk. He knows that any power from God given to the church is power that is given to thrash his kingdom. For this reason, the devil has been working overtime to convince pastors that the baptism of the Holy Spirit is too controversial to teach on. In fact, many gloss over the Holy Spirit altogether. This has resulted in a church that is sick and in bondage. What our churches need is teaching on the Holy Spirit, who He is, what He does, His fruit, and His gifts.

Unfortunately, if the church is being shielded from teaching on who the Holy Spirit is and what He does, the enemy has no problem sharing his thoughts with the church concerning who He is and what He does. The enemy will cause people to fear Him. This causes them to shy away from the one who gives the power to heal, liberate, and empower them to produce Kingdom fruit. The Holy Spirit is not controversial. He is not strange, nor is He someone to be feared. He is God. His power unleashed in our churches is key to the freedom of the church and advancement of God's Kingdom. Many in the church need a revelation of the Holy Spirit. Kathryn Kuhlman would implore those in her meetings to not grieve Him because He was all she had. He is all we have as well.

Too many do not understand the nature of the Holy Spirit, nor the moving of the Holy Spirit. This includes many pastors. If they did, they would not be so quick to cut Him off. For our services to effectively change lives, it is a necessity to make a comfortable place for the Holy Spirit's presence to come, and for Him to move.

Sadly, what we see is seeker-sensitive services. They boast of "doing church differently". Their goal is to reach groups of people who want no part of "religion". However, the method that they use to do this many times removes the Holy Spirit from their services. They substitute Him with a coffee shop and hip furniture. They have rock concert-like worship in dimly lit sanctuaries with smoke machines, cool lights, and lasers. They give twenty-six-minute messages with little scripture, crafted to make you feel good about you, and keep you comfortable and coming back to the weekly church production. This eye, ear, and mind candy draws seekers in droves, yet is ineffective in changing their lives. Emotional experiences and ambiance lie to the people, making them believe that this is God's presence.

But when we give the Holy Spirit rule and reign in our services, healing and deliverance happens. The dry are watered, the weary are refreshed, the Word is revealed, the church is empowered, emboldened, and evangelistic fires are lit. When the Holy Spirit has total rule and reign in our services, Christ is revealed to the lost, their spiritual state is revealed, they repent and are born again.

When the Holy Spirit has rule and reign, the church falls in love with God. The churches that do not allow the moving of the Spirit do well in making church members. The church may grow to be a mile wide. On the outside, these churches have the appearance of success.

However, being a church member does not mean you are a disciple of Christ!

The churches that pursue the Holy Spirit's presence are the ones who are successful in fulfilling the commission to make Christ disciples. If we are beholden to the Spirit of God, we are not beholden to man. Worship will be God-focused, and the Word will be full of truth, producing the change that will make us more Christ-like, more in love.

It is the Holy Spirit's presence in our church services that drives discipleship and changes lives. Long before smoke machines, laser light shows, state-of-the-art video backdrops, and concert sounds, the Holy Spirit was effective at drawing people to the Savior. We do not need new gimmicks; we simply need to break the box that we have kept the Holy Spirit in, allowing Him to have His way. It is and has always been the Holy Spirit that draws the people, teaches the people, and lights the people on fire to be a witness.

Chapter 15

Power Evangelism

The goal of every believer should be to imitate Christ in every way. Jesus is perfect theology. As imitators of Christ, we should also imitate the way He did evangelism. Jesus never debated, nor did He argue with people. Jesus healed the sick, raised the dead, cleansed the lepers and cast out demons. Jesus both preached the Kingdom of God and demonstrated the Kingdom with miracles, signs and wonders, and the people flocked to Him.

"And Jesus went throughout all the cities and villages, teaching in their synagogues and proclaiming the gospel of the kingdom and healing every disease and every affliction" (Matthew 9:35).

Jesus set the model for evangelism. John Wimber of the Vineyard movement coined the phrase, "power evangelism" to describe the model of evangelism that Jesus demonstrated. What exactly is power evangelism? Power evangelism is simply preaching the gospel with demonstrations of God's power. In scripture, we see that every time people are sent out to do evangelism, they are sent out to preach the gospel and demonstrate it with miracles, signs, and wonders. Not only do we see this in the ministry of Jesus, but we see it when Jesus sent out the seventy-two.

"After this, the Lord appointed seventy-two others and sent them on ahead of him, two by two, into every town and place where he himself was about to go. And he said to them, 'The

harvest is plentiful, but the laborers are few. Therefore pray earnestly to the Lord of the harvest to send out laborers into his harvest. Go your way; behold, I am sending you out as lambs in the midst of wolves. Carry no money bag, no knapsack, no sandals, and greet no one on the road. Whatever house you enter, first say, "Peace be to this house!" And if a son of peace is there, your peace will rest upon him. But if not, it will return to you. And remain in the same house, eating and drinking what they provide, for the laborer deserves his wages. Do not go from house to house. Whenever you enter a town and they receive you, eat what is set before you. Heal the sick in it and say to them, "The kingdom of God has come near to you""" (Luke10:1-9).

We see this again when Jesus sends out the twelve.

"These twelve Jesus sent out, instructing them, 'Go nowhere among the Gentiles and enter no town of the Samaritans, but go rather to the lost

sheep of the house of Israel. And proclaim as you go, saying, "The kingdom of heaven is at hand." Heal the sick, raise the dead, cleanse lepers, cast out demons. You received without paying; give without pay'" (Matthew 10:5-8).

In Mark 16:15-18, Jesus commissioned the disciples, that is you and I, to proclaim the gospel to all nations. He goes on to say that as we believers step out to make Him known, we would cast out devils, speak in other languages, and heal the sick.

"And he said to them, 'Go into all the world and proclaim the gospel to the whole creation. Whoever believes and is baptized will be saved, but whoever does not believe will be condemned. And these signs will accompany those who believe: in my name they will cast out demons; they will speak in new tongues; they will pick up serpents with their hands; and if they drink any deadly poison, it will not hurt them; they will lay their hands on the sick, and they will recover'" (Mark 16:15-18).

As we read through the four gospels, there is hardly a page where we do not read of Jesus functioning in supernatural ministry. It was miracles, signs and wonders that revealed Christ as the Messiah. We see this illustrated clearly in Matthew 11:2-6:

"Now when John heard in prison about the deeds of the Christ, he sent word by his disciples [3] and said to him, 'Are you the one who is to come, or shall we look for another?' And Jesus answered them, 'Go and tell John what you hear and see: the blind receive their sight and the lame walk, lepers are cleansed and the deaf hear, and the dead are raised up, and the poor have good news preached to them. And blessed is the one who is not offended by me'" (Matthew 11:2-6).

When John's disciples asked Jesus if He was the one that they've been waiting for, Jesus didn't respond by saying "Yup, I'm the guy"! His response was, "The blind receive their sight and the lame walk, lepers are cleansed and the deaf hear, and the dead are raised up, and the poor have good news preached to them." Jesus revealed Himself as Messiah by the works that He was doing. Jesus is still revealing who He is by the works He is doing through His body, the church!

Chapter 16

The People
I Couldn't Help

After receiving the Baptism of the Spirit, I was completely lit on fire to share the gospel. I would go out on the streets multiple nights a week to share Jesus with anyone who would listen to me.

I remember one night in particular, a young girl approached me. She was shaky and moving spastically. She was extremely disheveled and dirty. As she approached me, she asked me, "Mr. Preacher-man, can you get the devil out of me?"

Her name was Angela. Angela was an eighteen-year-old crack-addicted prostitute. It was evident that Angela was full of demons. I shared the gospel with her. She told me that her father was a minister, and she had been raised in the church. I led her to recommit her life to Christ and encouraged her to go home to her father. She walked away, shaky and spastic, seemingly exactly the same as when she approached me. She had asked me if I could get the devil out of her. The answer was no, I did not know how to get the devil out of her.

That encounter with Angela haunted me. Ministering in the inner city, I encountered countless broken people engaging in activities that break people. I would preach the gospel to them; many would pray to receive Christ through tears. These ministry encounters had all the appearances of being a life-changing moment in their lives. They would swear that they would come to church, but they never did. I would go back out on the street only to find these people still pimping, still prostituting, and still using drugs. I began to get discouraged. I knew there was something that I was missing. I began to cry out to God to show me what it was.

Soon after meeting Angela, I was invited to a large Christian event in my area. At this event, they were selling books, and as I was browsing through the books, one title caught my eye. It was a book by Derek Prince called, *They Shall Expel Demons*. I purchased the book, and that night I read testimony after testimony of people being set free from demonic bondage. I was seeing the people whom I felt powerless to help in the pages of that book. I began to read every book that I could get my hands to learn as much as I could about deliverance. As I began to discover the ministry of deliverance, my eyes opened to see things in the Word of God that I had not seen before.

Everywhere Jesus went, He healed the sick and He cast out demons. These accounts in the four gospels and Acts came alive to me. I was provoked to jealousy. I wanted to see people get set free! I then discovered Mark 16:17-18: "*And these signs will accompany those who believe: in my name they will cast out demons; they will speak in new tongues; they will pick up serpents with their hands; and if they drink any deadly poison, it will not hurt them; they will lay their hands on the sick, and they will recover.*"

It occurred to me, "I am a believer; therefore, I can cast out demons, and lay hands on the sick and they will recover!" Once I received this revelation, I held on to it for dear life, despite not seeing anyone healed or delivered. For ten years I prayed for people for healing and deliverance without seeing any results; then suddenly, it was like a dam burst and everything changed!

Chapter 17

In My Name They Will Cast Out Demons

I woke one morning and trudged into the living room. My wife announced to me that she was going to Texas for an inner healing conference. I told her if she was going, then so was I. In my wife's search for freedom, she stumbled across Gateway Church in Dallas, Texas. Gateway had a ministry they called "Freedom Ministry." They would go through a series of classes, and at the end of the cycle, they would have a conference-type event called "Kairos weekend." Amy and I had both read books on inner healing, but we had never gone through inner healing ministry. We really had no idea what we were getting ourselves into.

That weekend, we dealt with mother and father wounds and confessed forgiveness for those who have hurt us. We broke soul ties, generational curses, as well as inner vows and judgments. Each session built off the last. God was wrecking me in a beautiful way. I spent a good part of the weekend on my face crying as God was delivering me, confronting lies, and teaching my heart the truth.

At one point, the worship band played the song "How He Loves." As I sang that song, the presence of God came upon me so powerfully that I couldn't stand. As I laid on my face, I had one of the most intense encounters with the love of God that I have ever had; waves of God's love washed over me and through me. God was healing me with his love! The Lord spoke to me.

He said, "I have called you to minister this to others, as well as teach others to minister this." On the flight home, I told my wife what the Lord had spoken to me. She told me that the Lord had spoken the same thing to her.

Just one week later, Amy and I attended a worship event together. At the end of the service, a friend of mine approached me and asked if I'd pray for his friend to receive the baptism of the Holy Spirit. So, I laid my hands on him and asked Jesus to baptize him in the Spirit. Suddenly, this man began to shake, then he began to choke. The next thing I knew, he put his hands on his throat and began to try to strangle himself! I thought I had read every deliverance book on the planet but reading about manifesting demons and coming face to face with a manifesting demon are two different things!

I had very recently been promoted to the position of lead altar worker in my church. I was responsible for training the altar team. I was the "expert". Everyone on the team was there; they were watching me to see what I would do. The problem was, I didn't know what to do! On the outside, I had my feet set, with a steely-eyed look on my face. I looked very unintimidated. However, on the inside, I felt like a four-year-old girl crying for her mommy.

As I nervously looked at this man, I asked the Lord, "What is this?" Instantly, the word *suicide* came into my mind. I sharply said, "Spirit of suicide, come out of him!" Immediately, he began to shake harder. He then collapsed and began to cough violently. The demon came out of him, and with a big smile on his face, he began to pray in tongues!

Since that night, I have cast thousands of demons out of people. This ministry is vital to successful evangelism. We see throughout the four gospels that deliverance was a major part of the ministry of Christ. Deliverance is the foundation of the gospel! Jesus died and rose so that we could be delivered out of the kingdom of darkness and translated into the Kingdom of God! *"He has delivered us from the domain of darkness and transferred us to the kingdom of his beloved Son" (Colossians 1:13).*

Satan's greatest desire is to keep people from coming to a saving knowledge of Christ. When we engage in evangelism, we are literally crossing enemy lines, and going into the camp of the enemy. In doing this, inevitably you will eventually have a run-in with a demon. When most of us think of demonic manifestations, we imagine a person down on the ground, writhing.

Or perhaps we think of demons shrieking or causing the person to speak in a low guttural voice. Of course, demons do manifest in these ways. These are the obvious manifestations. But when doing evangelism, we often experience demonic manifestations without realizing it. There are some manifestations that are very subtle.

Incessant talking

You will encounter people who will not allow you to speak. When you begin to talk about Jesus, they suddenly develop diarrhea of the mouth! They will often say things like, "Oh, I love the Lord, I pray all the time... I don't know what I'd do without Him." When you try to share the gospel, the nervous chatter increases. The purpose is to get you to become frustrated and give up.

Blocking the ability to hear and see the truth

I remember years ago I was sharing the gospel with a guy. He was telling me his problems. I then shared the gospel and asked if he'd like to receive Christ. It was as if he did not hear a word I said. He again told me all his problems. I again shared the gospel with him. The cycle repeated. As he rehearsed his problems for the third time, the Lord spoke to me. He told me to bind the demon that had its hands over his ears and eyes.

I looked straight into his eyes and said, "In the name of Jesus, demon I bind you. In Jesus' name I command you to remove your hands from his eyes and ears!" I shared the gospel with him again. This time, he heard it and received Jesus as Savior. When I addressed the demon, it didn't faze the man in the least. It was as if he didn't hear a word I said. Without a doubt, the demon heard!

Debates or arguments

Early on, I would easily get sucked into arguments. Rarely, if ever, do these encounters produce Kingdom fruit. There are those who genuinely have questions. I will talk to these people all day long. However, there are those who have no desire to hear truth. We encounter these people often when doing street ministry. All they want to do is make you look bad, frustrate you, and take you away from those whom you would encounter that are receptive to the gospel. Jesus instructs us in Matthew 7:6 to not cast our pearls before swine. I refuse to argue or debate with a devil. If the Lord leads, I will take authority over the demon. If the Lord does not lead me in that way, I will share truth with them and exit the conversation. Keep in mind, it is our job to share truth; it is God's job to cause them to believe that truth.

Distraction in nature

I was ministering to a couple of guys on a city sidewalk. Suddenly, from literally out of nowhere, a swarm of wasps began to attack the two guys that I was ministering to. They were both stung. The wasps did not come near me. One of them was stung on his finger and the other on his arm. I asked the one who was stung on his finger to hold out his hand. I put my hand on it and commanded the venom out of his finger and the pain to leave in the name of Jesus. Within moments, all his pain was gone, and his finger was no longer swollen! I prayed for the other guy's arm, and he was also healed. What the devil meant for destruction; God worked for good! Their healed wasp stings opened their eyes to the reality of Christ. They heard the gospel, and both received Christ as their Lord and Savior!

Human distractions

I have found many times when I have approached a group to share the gospel, I am there for only one person. I remember one instance when I approached a group and began talking about the things of God, there was one girl out of that group who was locked on to what I was saying. While I spoke, her friends began to make fun of me. They kept it up despite their friend asking them to stop. I felt a holy boldness rise up on the inside of me, I turned to them and commanded them to be quiet in the name of Jesus. From then on, they kept quiet.

There are other times when I have not felt that boldness and have simply asked the person who is listening to step away from the crowd to continue the conversation without distraction. I remember ministering to a large group of

Muslims. The Lord had healed a few of them of back pain, causing them to be open to hearing the gospel. I began to share the gospel. When I mentioned the name of Jesus, one of their children who could not have been any more than five years old began to scream bloody murder! She started screaming, "Don't say that! Don't say that!" That caused the whole group to get stirred up, and the encounter fell apart.

Sudden freaking out

As I will share later, when I share the gospel, my approach is conversational. Many times, I'll strike up a conversation with a person about anything other than Jesus. I do this to help that person to become more relaxed. If we come in with our Jesus guns blazing, many times this will quickly abort the encounter. I remember a time when I was having an amazing conversation with someone about the Steelers. I began to swing the conversation towards spiritual things, and everything was going well until I mentioned the name of Jesus. As soon as I said the name of

Jesus, he released a barrage of obscenities. He went from completely normal to absolute lunatic in two and a half seconds! Some would say that that is mental illness. I say it is demonic possession!

Since we will encounter demons, it is important that we know how to deal with them.

"And Jesus came and said to them, *'All authority in heaven and on earth has been given to me. Go therefore and make disciples of all nations, baptizing them in the name of the Father and of the Son and of the Holy Spirit, teaching them to observe all that I have commanded you. And behold, I am with you always, to the end of the age'" (Matthew 28:18-20).*

Jesus, who is the head of the church, was given all authority in heaven and earth. If the head of the church was given authority, then the body that is connected to that head was given that same authority! Whatever is given to the head is given to the body! It is important that we understand this.

Here's a news flash, the devil is not afraid of Christians! Believe it or not, he also is not afraid of Christians who know they have authority. However, the devil is afraid of Christians who know they have authority *and use it!* Jesus went to the cross to destroy the works of the devil. As ambassadors of Christ, we are to function in that authority to enforce what Christ accomplished on the cross! The devil does not want to give up his territory, so we must make him.

"From the days of John the Baptist until now the kingdom of heaven has suffered violence, and the violent take it by force" (Matthew 11:12).

Understanding that we have authority over demons, and walking in it, is vital if we want to advance the Kingdom of God. Recently, the city where I live received the title: "the heroin capital of the world." Looking with different eyes, a former pastor of mine used to refer to Butler,

Pennsylvania as "the pearl of the world," and I agree with him!

When I do street ministry, I often encounter many who are addicted. I could share with you story after story of the people I have met who received deliverance on the street, who came to Jesus as a result. When Jesus shows up on the scene and sets people free from demons, they follow Him. These people, many times, follow God with a red hot passion and do much damage to Satan's kingdom! We see this with Mary Magdalene.

"Soon afterward he went on through cities and villages, proclaiming and bringing the good news of the kingdom of God. And the twelve were with him, and also some women who had been healed of evil spirits and infirmities: Mary, called Magdalene, from whom seven demons had gone out" (Luke 8:1-2).

I will close this chapter with a perfect example of the necessity of deliverance. One night while doing street ministry, I encountered a woman who was very drunk. She could hardly stand, and her words were slurred. I asked if I could pray for her to which she said yes. I put my hand on her head and commanded the spirit of drunkenness to leave her, in the name of Jesus. There was no hardcore demonic manifestation.

As I commanded, she stood there with her head down. I then asked, "Do you still feel drunk?" She lifted her head, and with a puzzled look on her face, replied without slurring her speech, "No I don't." Immediately she was sober! I noticed she had scoliosis. I prayed for her back and felt her spine straighten under my hand. I then shared the gospel with her.

Through tears, she recommitted her life to Christ! As it turned out, 10 years earlier she had been married to a pastor who was a narcissist. He abused her both physically and emotionally. She finally went to the leaders of the church. Long story short, it was all turned around on her, and she was forced out of the church. She became bitter with the church and with God and began to drink to stifle her pain. What a beautiful thing to see God's faithfulness towards this woman! Jesus went into the muck and mire after her, to break her out of the demonic prison of drunkenness, to heal her body, to reveal His love, and restore her soul!

Chapter 18

Activated

When I was nine years old, I was at Wednesday night children's Bible study. One Wednesday, as I was waiting for my mom to pick me up, I was approached by a man in my church who told me that Pastor Jonathan would like to pray for me. Pastor Jonathan was a Honduran pastor. My church supported his church. He was in the United States for the week.

My first thought was, "You must have the wrong kid. The pastor's kid is over there." I was probably the most broken kid in the place. Sure enough, it was me. I remember him placing his hand on my head and fervently praying in Spanish. The translator began to translate what he was prophesying over me.

Pastor Jonathan prophesied that I would be a great man of God, if I would keep my eyes upon the Lord. He prophesied that God was giving me a miracle ministry and that many would come to salvation through my life. As I grew up, I grew away from God and eventually walked away completely.

As deep in sin as I was, I never forgot that prophetic word. It was like a rope tied around my waist that was constantly trying to pull me back to God. It always baffled me that he would prophesy these things over me. I was such a mess, and I was sure that God could not use a mess. I walked through ten years of extreme darkness, and then God got a hold of my heart.

As I said earlier, I began going to a Dutch Reformed church. Pastor Steve of that church immediately began to mentor me. He would try to pound it into my head that God no longer heals through people; he even gave me a list of T.V. preachers that I absolutely should not watch. But it was too late; I had grown up in a church where miracles, signs, and wonders were a regular occurrence.

Even as a spiritual infant, I understood that Pastor Steve only knew what he knew. Benny Hinn was at the top of his list! I loved to watch Benny Hinn. As the people would come forward to testify of being healed, I would weep as they shared their stories. From early on in my walk with God, my daily prayer was that God would use me to heal the sick. I was so drawn to people being set free because I knew all too well what bondage felt like.

Six months after God saved me, He moved me out of the Dutch Reformed church and into a small charismatic church. That is where I met

Phil. The first time I met Phil, he prayed over me. As he prayed, he began to prophesy, verbatim, everything that Pastor Jonathan prophesied over me. For the next two years, at almost every gathering I attended, God would send people to me who did not know me but would prophesy that I would function in a healing and miracle ministry. Through prophetic ministry, I was positive that God had called me to heal the sick!

As I shared in chapter seventeen, I began to see many people delivered from demons. I would see people receive physical healing when the sickness was demonically rooted. However, there were plenty of people whom I prayed for who were not healed. Though I had only seen a few healed, I was still convinced that healing was to be a big part of my ministry. God began to remind me of the prophetic words I had received a decade ago. I began to seek God for the healing component I was missing.

One day I was speaking with my spiritual mom. She told me that she was going to be in PA to go to a conference. I asked what conference it was. The conference was called, "Voice of the Apostles," Randy Clark's ministry. I had gone to a few meetings as a new believer. At that point in my walk with God, I had not been baptized in the Spirit and was still pretty afraid of him.

By this time, I had gone to Bible school twice and thought I was an expert on what a move of the Spirit looked like. I was positive that those people were "off". I would often make fun of Randy Clark's meetings. I would say, "You see more flesh at a Randy Clark meeting than you'd see at a nudist colony". However, in the days that followed that conversation with my spiritual mom, I began to feel a pull to go to the conference. I went back and forth, but I knew that God had something for me there.

I went to the conference with extreme apprehension. I had never experienced such a strong presence of God. Despite feeling God's presence, as the different ministers spoke, I listened intently, trying to pick the messages apart to find the heresy...but heard none. A South Korean pastor named Che' Ahn got up to speak. He began to share on "power evangelism". He told story after story of going out on the street, praying for the sick, preaching the gospel, and leading people to Jesus. I was on the edge of my seat as I listened to him.

As he spoke, my heart was burning! This is what I was made to do! The Lord spoke to me, saying, "I want you to have him pray for you." I told my wife what God had spoken to me, and her reply was, "Good luck with that." The problem with this was that these guys would preach and either minister from the platform or go backstage. I wasn't sure how meeting him could happen.

After his message, my wife and I went downstairs to the bookstore. As we were looking through the books, my wife nudged me and said, "Kevin, look!" Standing right next to me was Che' Ahn. I waited for him to finish his conversation and approached him. I told him that I felt like I was to have him pray for me. He asked what I wanted. I told him, "I want everything you've got." He then told me to walk with him. We walked out of the bookstore into the hallway. There were roughly five thousand people at this conference. During the breaks, at least three thousand people were in this hallway.

As we walked, Che' Ahn placed his hand on my stomach and said, "Take it!" I have never grabbed a hold of a power line, but I think I know what it feels like to do so. When he said, "Take it", the power of God surged through my body. I immediately dropped and began to shake under the power of God. My wife stood in front of me, trying to block people from stepping on me.

I can still remember her looking down on me with an annoyed look on her face saying, "Would you get up already!" I couldn't move! Eventually, I peeled myself up off the floor and made it back to my seat. In my ten years of being a Christian, I had never felt the power of God like I did at that moment. At the time, I had no idea that that encounter would catapult me into my destiny.

A week after the conference, my wife and I were laying in bed watching TV. My wife told me that she had been having pain in her side for a couple of weeks, and it wasn't going away. She asked me if I'd pray for her. I put my hand on her side, not really expecting anything to happen. I commanded the pain to leave in the name of Jesus. As I prayed, I could feel my hand getting hot. That's when she said, "It feels like there is a heating pad on the inside of me." When I finished praying, she told me that her pain was gone. I was amazed!

The next day I went to work where I met a man named Vince. A few years earlier, Vince had been in a car accident. In the accident, his knee was shattered. Vince was only forty-two years old, so they didn't want to do knee replacement surgery. The doctors feared that it would wear out and he would need another, and eventually be in a wheelchair.

Vince then told me that his wife had died a year earlier, leaving him with a fourteen-year-old daughter and a five-year-old son. He began to cry as he told me that he was unable to play with his son or take care of him. I asked if I could pray for him. He said, "At this point, I'm willing to try anything." I put my hand on his knee and commanded it to come back together in the name of Jesus. Suddenly, I began to feel his knee crack and pop. I could feel the bones in his knee move under my hand. When I was done, Vince jumped to his feet and began to jump up and down on the leg with the knee that had been shattered.

At that point, I told him, "Ya know Vince, what God just did for your knee is nothing compared to what He wants to do for your heart!" I then shared the gospel with him. When I was done, Vince said, "I never believed in all that religious crap, but I do now. I believe every word you just said. I need Jesus!" I then led Vince to Christ. I got in my car with my mind completely blown over what I just saw. There was no debating. I didn't have to convince him of anything. I prayed, God healed him, his eyes were opened to Christ, and he received Him as Savior. That was power evangelism. It was easy! That day everything changed.

Chapter 19

You Will Lay Hands On the Sick, and They Will Recover

Since that day, I have seen God heal thousands of people. Many of these healings resulted in the person giving their lives to Christ. When God began to use me to heal the sick, I at once began to understand why healing was such a large part of Christ's ministry. Over the last decade, healing has been my greatest tool as it pertains to leading atheists, agnostics, as well as those of other religions to

Christ! Witnessing to these groups can be one of the most frustrating things a Christian can do. There are some people who have made up their minds that they will not believe a word you say. When you quote scripture, they tell you that the Bible was written by men. If you try to debate them, whether you disprove their argument or not, they will switch their argument. If you share your testimony, they'll say, "It's good that you were able to change yourself." It is annoying! They can argue with what you say all day long, but when they have a tangible encounter with God, most times that will shut their mouths and open their ears.

I remember meeting a woman at a wedding years ago. As soon as I saw her, I felt that God wanted me to talk to her. Eventually, our paths crossed at the punch bowl, and we began to chat. Her name was Angela. I quickly learned that Angela was an atheist. She told me that the Bible was a bunch of stories. She asked me if I really believed in a talking snake, a boat that held two of every living animal, a parting sea, a man swallowed by a whale. Angela told me that she couldn't bring herself to believe in a God that she couldn't see, feel, or touch. I then asked her, "What if you could feel God?"

She said, "I want to believe in God. If I could feel Him, then I'd believe in Him." I then asked her to give me her hands and close her eyes, which she did. I invited the Holy Spirit to come and touch her. Immediately, I could feel a strong presence of God, and she could as well! She began to tremble. I asked her if she could feel His presence, to which she nodded her head. I felt to ask if she had pain in her body.

Without opening her eyes, she told me that she has constant pain at the top of her stomach, for which the doctors could not find a cause. I commanded an afflicting spirit to come out of her. Immediately her upper torso began to move as if something was coming up from inside of her. She opened her mouth and let out a gasp. She told me that when I commanded it out it felt as if a ball came up from the place where she was having pain. It came up into her throat and out of her mouth when she gasped. All her pain was gone! I then asked her if she was still an atheist. She told me, "Absolutely not." I shared the gospel with her, and she prayed to receive Jesus as her Savior.

Over the last ten years, I have seen thousands of people healed of various sicknesses and pain, resulting in their repenting of their sins, and giving their lives to Christ. I now travel the country heralding the message: If I can do this, then so can you!

Like deliverance, many of us have viewed the ministry of healing as being for the super anointed, or only for "top tier" Christians. Mark 16:17 says, *"These signs will follow them who believe."* The only qualification for healing the sick is that you be born again. Some of us miss the fact that when you received Christ as Savior, the same Holy Spirit that empowered Him took up residence in you. The same authority that

Christ walked in is available for you to walk in as part of Christ's body!

I have had many say they do not have a healing gift. But do you realize that when the Spirit of God took up residence in you, He brought all nine gifts with Him? Right now, all nine gifts of the Holy Spirit are in you, ready to manifest when needed. If you encounter someone who needs a healing in their body for Christ to be revealed, God is not up in heaven saying, "Sorry, you don't have a healing gift. I can't help you out."

A few years ago, I visited a woman for work who had severe hip issues. She could barely walk with the use of a walker. She invited me into her living room. She introduced me to her nephew Antonio, who grunted, "Hi". He would not even look at me. Antonio had to be six foot four and two hundred and fifty pounds. He looked very angry and intimidating. As I scanned my surroundings, I noticed Christian books on her bookshelf and a tattered Bible on her end table. I saw that she was a Christian, so eventually we began to talk about the things of God. At a point in the conversation, she turned to her nephew and said, "Antonio was raised in church but has walked away from God. Now he says he's an atheist."

When she said this, I heard the Lord say, "Grow his leg out". Without giving it a second thought, I jumped out of my chair, got onto my knees, grabbed his tree-trunk legs, and held them up. I'm not sure who was more surprised by what I was doing, me or him! He looked shocked; he was speechless! I commanded his leg to grow in the name of Jesus. Immediately his leg grew. I put his leg down, expecting him to kick me through the wall. Instead, he leaned forward with his head down and stayed in that position for a moment.

When he straightened himself, I noticed tears running down his cheeks. He looked at his aunt and said, "Auntie, my back doesn't hurt anymore." Suddenly emboldened, I said,

"Antonio, now you know that God is real, and what you learned about Christ dying on the cross is true, right?" He nodded his head and said, "Yes, sir." I then said, "If what you heard about Christ dying on the cross for your sin is true, then what you heard about hell is also true. You have a decision to make. Are you going to receive Christ, or are you going to deny Him?"

Without hesitation and through tears, he replied, "I need Jesus." I led him in a prayer to receive Christ and said, "Now it's time to get to work." I told him, "Now you're going to pray for your aunt's hip." He gave me a panicked look and said, "I don't know how." I told him to put his hand on her hip and command her hip to be healed in the name of Jesus. He did what I said, and his hand began to tremble as he commanded her hip to be healed. When he was done, his aunt stood up on her own and walked across the room perfectly normal and pain-free! Antonio was saved for a minute and twenty seconds, yet God used him to heal his aunt.

Years ago, I was one of the lead teachers in my church's children's ministry. I taught elementary-aged children. Being an evangelist, my teaching many times had an evangelistic bent. I taught them how to share their faith and how to hear from God. I taught them about the Holy Spirit, the baptism of the Spirit and how to pray for the sick. Every Sunday, I would always leave time at the end for ministry. I wouldn't pray for them; they would pray for each other. Healings were a regular occurrence in that classroom. I would ask if anyone needed prayer. If someone did need prayer, they would all want to be the one to pray.

I remember one little girl named Jennifer asked for prayer because she had fallen off her bike, resulting in a concussion. A month later she still had a constant headache. I asked who would like to pray. I chose eight-year-old Abby to pray. I told her to command trauma to leave. Abby put her hand on Jennifer's head, and authoritatively said, "In the name of Jesus, trauma leave!" Jennifer said that it felt as if someone put a vacuum up to her head and sucked the headache out! She never had another headache after that.

Another little girl named Cadence asked to pray for her grandfather, who had been bitten on the wrist by a brown recluse spider. This resulted in an infection that was not healing. He said yes to her, not really believing that anything would happen. Cadence prayed the way that she had been taught to pray. As she prayed, her grandfather felt a warm electric feeling in his wrist. When she was done, all his pain was gone. That night he changed his bandage to find that the infection was gone, and brand-new pink skin was covering what had been a wound!

Finally, I was approached by a woman named Sharon in my church who had a stroke, causing her foot to turn in. She had to use a cane and was very unstable. She asked if I'd pray for her foot to straighten out. Eleven-year-old Shay was close by, so I called her over. I told her that I wanted her to pray for Sharon's foot to straighten out. I could tell that Sharon was disappointed with this; she wanted me to pray.

Without hesitation, Shay dropped to her knees, grabbed Sharon's foot, and sharply said, "In the name of Jesus, foot straighten out!" There was an incredibly strong presence of God as she prayed. However, there was no noticeable change. I explained that sometimes healing is not always immediate. Shay left and I went out in the hall. As I was talking to a friend, Sharon walked past me with her cane over her shoulder! I stopped her and asked what happened. She said, "A few minutes after you guys left, my foot straightened out, and all of the pain and weakness left!"

I could write hundreds of stories of others who were not "ministry professionals," who simply took God at His word and stepped out in authority, putting a demand on the power of the Holy Spirit and saw incredible results! Why not you? Over the next few chapters, I will focus on the nuts and bolts of the ministry of healing, because it is such a game-changer when it comes to winning the lost.

Chapter 20

The Foundation of Successful Healing Ministry

Years ago, I was invited to a church to do a conference on the Holy Spirit. I was to teach on the baptism of the Holy Spirit, healing, and deliverance. The pastor picked me up from the airport and we went to have lunch. While at lunch, we began talking about healing. He was adamant that healing was not God's will for everyone. His daughter had pulmonary fibrosis. She had not been healed despite his prayers, so he decided that healing was not always God's will.

Throughout our conversation, he mentioned over and over how he had taught through the Word, verse by verse, at least 15 times. He prided himself on his vast Bible knowledge. I decided that I would not try to challenge him on this. I had to be with him for the weekend, and I knew that I would not win a debate with him. I decided to preserve unity.

To avoid confusion and conflict, I decided to scratch my teaching on healing. Had I taught on God's will to heal, he may have confronted me in the pulpit and would have retaught everything I said. Though I didn't teach on healing, I prayed for healing, and the majority were healed. For those who were not healed, I pulled the microphone away from my mouth and whispered, "It is absolutely God's will that you be healed! Stand on God's Word. Confess His Word over your body. Do not entertain anything that is contrary to healing being God's will!"

Randy Clark once said, "Do not lower God's Word to the level of your experience but raise your expectation to the level of God's Word." Prior to God using me in healing, I was guilty of lowering God's Word to my level of experience. I felt as if I needed to defend God for someone not receiving healing. I would say things like, "God is using your sickness to bring Him glory." or, "God is keeping you humble and dependent on Him through your sickness." The worst one was, "If God were to heal you, you'd start living like a Viking again."

I remember the day God opened my eyes to truth. I was reading and meditating *on 1 John 3:8: "The reason the Son of God appeared was to destroy the works of the devil."* I then had a vision. In this vision, I saw Adam and Eve in the garden. They had perfect communion with God. They lacked nothing. There was no sickness, death, disease, or bondage. In this vision, I saw Satan slither in to tempt Adam and Eve with the fruit of the Tree of Knowledge of Good and Evil. As soon as Adam touched the forbidden fruit, sin entered the world, setting off a chain reaction of destruction.

At this point in the vision, I saw a tiny seed. Written on this seed was the word sin. This seed was dropped into the ground and covered with dirt. From that seed, a tree grew. Written in the roots of this tree was the word sin. On this tree hung fruit. Written on the fruit were the words sickness, death, disease, bondage, poverty. Suddenly in this vision, Jesus appeared with an ax. He approached the tree and began hacking away at the roots of the sin tree. The tree then fell, withered, and died, as did the fruit of the sin tree.

It occurred to me that the work of the devil is sin. If Jesus died on the cross to deal with sin, then He came to deal with the fruit of Sin! Jesus died to heal our sickness! This revelation changed everything. From that point on it no longer mattered if I saw someone healed or not. I was convinced that healing is always God's will.

This must be our foundational belief if we will be successful in healing the sick.

There is a law of faith that is found in Matthew 21:21: *"And Jesus answered them, 'Truly, I say to you, if you have faith and do not doubt, you will not only do what has been done to the fig tree, but even if you say to this mountain, "Be taken up and thrown into the sea," it will happen'"* (Matthew 21:21).

"Have faith, and do not doubt" is the law of faith. This must be the foundation from which we pray. If it is God's will to heal some, but for others His will is sickness, how would it be possible to have faith and not doubt? It would be impossible to pray in faith if God's will vacillates. Either His will is healing or not. God is not double-minded as some make Him out to be. If we believe that sickness is God's will, we are equating Him with the thief who, according to John 10:10 comes to kill, steal and destroy. In the Lord's prayer, we are instructed to pray "...on earth as it is in heaven." There is no sickness in heaven. Jesus came so that we might have abundant life. Sickness is completely void of abundance. God is our Abba, which means papa or daddy. He is a warm, loving papa. He desires good for those who are His. A warm, loving papa does not punish His children with sickness. He doesn't teach them lessons with sickness. He doesn't keep them obedient with sickness, nor does He keep them connected to the Kingdom by sickness. A healed body brings Him far more glory than a sick body!

"Surely he has borne our griefs and carried our sorrows; yet we esteemed him stricken, smitten by God, and afflicted. But he was pierced for our transgressions; he was crushed for our iniquities; upon him was the chastisement that brought us peace, and with his wounds we are healed" (Isaiah 53:4-5).

In the Hebrew language, "griefs" can be translated as *sickness*, and the word "sorrows" can be translated as *pains*. Isaiah 53 can be read like this: *Surely, He has borne our griefs and carried our sicknesses*. The simplest way to break it down is this: God is good, and sickness is bad. The blood of Jesus purchased your healing. It is the provision for everything you need!

You Have Authority!

Authoritative prayers are effective prayers. As stated in the previous chapter, Jesus came to destroy the work of the devil. Sickness is the work of the devil. 2 Corinthians 5:20 declares that we are ambassadors of Christ. In other words, we are his representatives on the earth.

In Mark 16:15-18, Christ commissioned us to preach the gospel, cast out devils, and heal the sick. At that time, the church was delegated to carry on His earthly ministry. From that point on, our job has been to enforce all that was done on the cross. The entire church has been given the power and authority to do so. The point of the last chapter was to prove God's will to heal. Success in healing the sick is not dependent on how many scriptures you can quote while praying, or how loud you are. God's willingness to answer your prayer does not at all depend on how spiritual you sound, but it does depend on if you believe that what your saying is true, and what you command will happen. Through Christ, you have been given authority over sickness and demons. Many in the church do not understand our authority. If we did, we would not tolerate what we tolerate. We have not received partial authority, but we have received all authority.

Years ago, I had a friend named Rick. Rick had eighty percent hearing loss. I prayed for Rick's ears. I placed my hands on them and commanded them to open in Jesus' name, and they popped open! Months later, I asked Rick how his hearing was. He told me how amazing it is to hear the sound that the light switch makes when you flick it on, or how wonderful it is to wake in the morning and hear the birds singing outside!

He then told me that there were a few times that he would feel his ears starting to close. He told me that he would use his authority in Christ to command his ears to open, and immediately they did! There have been many instances where I have prayed for people and asked them how they felt, to have them tell me there was no difference. The devil is stubborn. He does not want to give up his ground. However, I too am stubborn in my belief that Jesus purchased healing with His blood.

Many times, as I continued to assert my authority over sickness or pain, healing has come. When praying for the sick, we must remember that the Greater One lives in us. "Little children, you are from God and have overcome them, for he who is in you is greater than he who is in the world" (John 4:4).

His power in us isn't just barely greater, His power in us is infinitely greater than any other power! *"For in him the whole fullness of deity dwells bodily, and you have been filled in him, who is the head of all rule and authority"* *(Colossians 2:9-10).* As I said earlier, the devil is not afraid of Christians. Nor is the devil afraid of Christians who know they have authority. The devil is afraid of Christians who know they have authority and use it! You will see the sick healed and demons leave when you start praying like you believe that sickness and demons must do what you say in Jesus' name.

A few months ago, I was in Hagerstown, MD to do a series of meetings. At one meeting, I noticed a young girl who was dressed in a black leather skirt, shirt, and jacket. She had pin-straight black hair, thick black eyeliner, black lipstick, and piercings all over her face. Her name was Danielle. Hanging from Danielle's neck was a pentagram necklace. I approached her and asked her if she was a witch. She said that she was. I asked her what she was doing at the meeting. She told me that she came with her grandmother so her grandmother wouldn't have to drive alone. This was one of the most powerful meetings that I have ever been a part of. People were wandering in off the street, getting healed, delivered, and receiving Christ! Literally, every person who came forward was delivered of demonic oppression and healed.

Finally, two kids came forward who wanted deliverance because they had been involved in a satanic ritual. Throughout the night I had felt that God wanted me to wait to confront Danielle concerning the witchcraft. When the two kids came forward, I felt like God gave me the go-ahead. I looked at Danielle and asked, "Don't you think you should come forward?" She replied, "I'm not going up there. You terrify me." I told her, "It isn't me who terrifies you. The demons in you are terrified of the Jesus in me." The Lord began to speak to me about her. I began to say what God was showing me. "You deal with debilitating panic and anxiety, depression, suicidal thoughts, insomnia, racing thoughts, and you hear voices, right?" She nodded her head and said, "Yes, I do."

I told her, "I have good news and bad news. I'll give you the bad news first. You have demons in you because of the witchcraft you've practiced. What you are dealing with will not get any better but will only get worse. Here's the good news. I know how to get those demons out of you!" I then said, "You have watched person after person come forward, get delivered, and healed. Now you know that Jesus is real and powerful, right?" She nodded her head. I then told her that God brought her here to set her free. I told her, "The foundation of your freedom is a relationship with Jesus. He died on the cross so that every sin you have ever committed could be forgiven if you are willing to turn from them and receive Christ as your Savior."

I then asked if she would like to receive Christ. She shrugged her shoulders and said, "I guess." I told her that I didn't want to pray with her unless she truly was ready to give her life to

Christ and pursue Him. I then knelt on the seat in front of her and asked for her hands. She then put her hands in mine.

I simply said, "Come Holy Spirit." Immediately, God's presence came upon us both. I could feel His presence stronger than I had ever felt when praying for someone. I asked Danielle, "Do you feel Him?" "This is the most beautiful feeling I have ever felt," she replied. I told her, "This is the Jesus who has come for you."

I then asked again, "Would you like to receive Jesus?" She took a moment, then she said, "Yes, I would like to receive Jesus Christ as my Lord and Savior." I prayed for her to receive Christ. As soon as I led her to Christ, I then sharply commanded, "Now come out in the name of Jesus!" She immediately began to shake. She threw her head back, opened her mouth wide and began growling, coughing, and releasing deep breaths. God saved her and cleaned her out! After she was delivered, Danielle looked up at me with sparkling bright brown eyes and said,

"Mr. Kevin, does this mean when I die, that I'll go to heaven?" I said, "Yes, you'll go to heaven. Follow Jesus."

A few weeks later, I received a message from her father. He wrote, "I want to thank you. You saved my daughter's life." He told me that she had tried to kill herself five times over the past few months, but she is now a brand-new person! Danielle told me that as soon as I looked at her, her whole body began to tremble. At the name of Jesus, every knee will bow!

Chapter 22

How to Pray
for the Sick

We have discussed that God is willing and able to heal. We have discussed our authority to heal. Finally, in this chapter, we will discuss how to heal the sick. I think one of the most important things that we can do before praying for a person for healing is to interview the person. If I have the time to do so, I will ask key questions, such as:

- What is your condition?

- What specifically does this condition affect?
- How long have you had this condition?
- What caused your condition?
- What were the circumstances in your life around the time that this condition began?
- Does (or did) any other family members have this same condition?
- On a scale of one to ten, what is your pain level?

By asking these key questions, I can determine how I will pray for the individual. I have found that many times there are roots to sickness that must be dealt with to effectively deal with the fruit. Depending on the answers I get to these questions, I know if I need to lead them in prayers of forgiveness towards those who have abused, abandoned, or betrayed them.

For instance, if a person tells me that the pain they are experiencing came because of abuse they had suffered, I will lead them to forgive their abuser. If someone tells me that they found out their husband was cheating on them and a week later they developed pain or sickness, I will pray for them to forgive their husband.

I remember getting a message from a woman requesting prayer who had severe fibromyalgia, a bulging disc, and degeneration in her spine. I prayed for her over the phone. When done, I asked if there was any difference to which she said there was no difference. I prayed again, still no change. I asked her if she had ever been abused. She told me that she was raped when she was fourteen. I led her to forgive the man who had abused her. I prayed again and she was completely healed.

With these questions, I can determine if the person requires deliverance for healing. Just about every time sickness or pain began after a trauma, a spirit of trauma must be dealt with. I have found that the spirit of trauma does not travel alone. Trauma holds the door open for spirits of pain, affliction, infirmity, and sickness.

I remember meeting with a woman who had every kind of arthritis that a person could possibly have. I asked her about the circumstances of her life around the time when she was first diagnosed with arthritis. She told me that when she was twelve her father suddenly died. She had been extremely close to him. His death was very difficult for her. She told me that a couple of weeks later she began to experience terrible pain in her joints. A month after his death she was diagnosed with juvenile arthritis. I led her in a prayer to renounce trauma, pain, affliction, infirmity, and arthritis. She began to feel electricity in all her joints. I commanded those demons out, and she told me that she could feel as if something was being pulled out of her joints. After receiving deliverance, she stood up and walked for completely pain-free for the first time in thirty years!

The reason I ask about family history is to determine if the sickness is the effect of a generational curse. I have seen many times that this is the case. One of my favorite healing stories happened when praying for a woman's arthritic shoulder. She told me that her mother, aunts, and sisters had the same condition as her. I led her in a prayer of repentance for any sin committed in her generational line that opened the door to the generational curse of shoulder issues. When she said, "I now break the curse of shoulder pain off of me and my children in Jesus' name!" her pain left.

Suddenly we heard, "Woah!" When she broke the curse, her daughter who was across the room said her shoulder popped and all her shoulder pain left!

There are times when I have felt led to ask about participation in witchcraft, either by themself or their family. I have done a lot of ministry in Honduras and have found witchcraft to be a leading factor in causing sickness and preventing healing.

Another hindrance to healing is spoken curses. Many times, in the interview process you can get a good feel for a person's self-perception. Not too long ago, I was praying for the sick in a meeting. I called out a word of knowledge for lower back pain. Three women came forward. Two of the women were immediately healed. The third said, "I knew I wouldn't be healed; I'm hopeless." Every word that came out of this woman's mouth was a curse. Her self-hatred was oozing out of her mouth.

Finally, I told her, "You will not be healed until you stop agreeing with the devil. The devil says you're hopeless, the devil says you're worthless. God says He is the God of all hope, and that you were worth His life. You need to decide whose word you will believe. Will you believe the devil, the father of lies? Or will you believe Jesus who is the truth?" She chose Jesus. I led her in a prayer to repent for speaking Satan's word over her life. We broke the curses she pronounced over herself and prayed again. Not only was her back healed, but her shoulder and her stomach were also healed!

Once I have determined what the root of the sickness is (if there is one), I will lead them in prayers of forgiveness, prayers to break generational curses, prayers of repentance, etc. At this point, I will deal with any demonic spirits that would hinder healing. I have found that after dealing with the root of the issue, that the pain or sickness is healed, or the symptoms are greatly reduced.

The next step is to pray for the healing of any body part that needs to be healed. When appropriate, I will place my hand on the body part that needs healing. When praying for women, I will take their hand, put my hand on their head, or have them place their hand on the area that needs healed, and I will touch their elbow.

Again, I will not just plow into prayer. At this point, I will invite the Holy Spirit to manifest His presence, and I will wait on Him. Many times, people will begin to feel heat or electricity in an area where they need to be healed. At this point, I will move into commanding prayer. "In the name of Jesus, I command this knee to be healed." I will be specific in what I want healed. "Knee, be healed. Tendons and ligaments, be healed. Cartilage, be formed. Muscles, be strengthened." I will then ask if they sense any change. If so, I will ask again what their pain level is on a scale of one to ten. If they say they have no pain, I will ask them to do something that they couldn't do. If they find that they still have pain, I'll pray again. There are many times that the pain level will drop. I will continue to pray until the pain or sickness disappears completely, symptoms are no longer present, or I feel released by the Holy Spirit to stop praying.

Many of us have been taught to pray with our eyes closed. When we pray, we should pray with our eyes open! My wife is highly anointed for heart healing. Most times, she will place her hands on the woman, close her eyes and begin to pray softly. People rarely fall when she prays for them; instead, they cry. One Sunday morning, a woman came up for prayer and Amy did her usual thing. She placed her hand on the woman's head, closed her eyes and began to pray softly. Suddenly, she was no longer feeling the woman's head. She heard a thud. Amy opened her eyes to find the woman on the floor. Had Amy's eyes been open, she could have potentially caught her or at least broken her fall. Amy now prays with her eyes open!

If you have invited the Holy Spirit to come and He is touching someone powerfully, then you want to keep quiet and allow Him to work. Many times, when the Holy Spirit is touching someone, they will begin to cry, tremble, or sweat. There are times when you will see a person's eyelids fluttering, they will sway, or fall out in the Spirit. When our eyes are open, we can see what the Spirit is doing and flow with Him.

Chapter 23

The Culture
We Create

Ever since my children were old enough to understand, whenever I would go out to do street ministry, I would purposely tell my children, "Daddy is going out to tell people about Jesus."

My purpose for doing this was to make sharing the gospel a normal, natural part of our lives. Christ followers are who we are, telling people about Jesus is what we do. I purposed to model this in front of them. One evening while having dinner, my son Joshua asked, "Daddy, what's the big deal about healing?" My daughter Anna then chimed in, "Yeah, why does everyone get so surprised by it?" I thought to myself, "Praise God, my plan is working!"

Just like I strived to create a culture of evangelism in my home, we should strive to create an evangelistic culture in our churches. This is done by emphasizing evangelism as much as anything else. For most, the bulk of evangelistic training doesn't go beyond the training one would get for church outreach events such as Easter egg hunts and Christmas pageants. There is nothing wrong with church events that draw the lost; however, we encounter people non-stop in our daily lives. Equipping the saints evangelistically should be an ongoing focus, with the push being, "Your *life* is a mission for God. Live your life as an outreach."

There should be constant encouragement to get out of our four walls and use what has been learned, but there should also be a platform for the people to share what God has done. Evangelism should be celebrated! Weekly testimonies cause faith to increase. It causes those who have been timid to be emboldened. It will cause people to become jealous for God to work through them. It will create an excited buzz in the church. Passion for God will increase as people experience His love and power poured out through them to others.

Lastly, evangelism is the cure for a stagnant church. A stagnant church is a church turned inward. As you turn your focus outward and keep it there, there will be a stirring in the church as they see God moving. The result will be that your church will grow!

Conclusion

"When he saw the crowds, he had compassion for them, because they were harassed and helpless, like sheep without a shepherd. Then he said to his disciples, 'The harvest is plentiful, but the laborers are few; therefore pray earnestly to the Lord of the harvest to send out laborers into his harvest'" (Matthew 9:36-38).

The world is broken more than we know. Sin has ravaged the world. The devil is killing, stealing, and destroying. The Lord is calling His church out of its sterile bubble. He is calling Bible studies out to the streets! He is calling intercessory prayer groups to the streets to do what they have been praying for God to do! He is calling churches to no longer sit back and wait for sinners to come to them, but to follow the biblical model of seeking and saving that which is lost by going out into the highways and byways!

The fields are white! Hearts are ripe to be harvested!

Last week, I saw a vision of America as one big wheat field. I saw no states, just wheat. I then saw the sickle of the Lord sweep across the nation. I heard Him say, "Where are my workers who will go to the fields to gather the harvest!" The Lord is still asking, "Whom shall I send, who will go?" How will you answer? Will you allow yourself to feel uncomfortable for the cause of Christ? Or Is your comfort more important than a soul in hell? That's a tough question, but it is reality.

What is this life anyway in the light of eternity? The only thing you'll do in this life that will matter in eternity is what you did to populate heaven. Use your time wisely.

Visit Kevin's website for more:

setfreeweekends.com

Made in the USA
Middletown, DE
02 September 2024

60245613R00126